Words for Our Lives

THE SPIRITUAL WORDS OF MATTHEW THE POOR

VOLUME 2

ANCIENT FAITH PUBLISHING

✠

CHESTERTON, INDIANA

Words for Our Lives:
The Spiritual Words of Matthew the Poor, Volume 2

English translation copyright © 2016 by James Helmy

Published by:
    Ancient Faith Publishing
     A division of Ancient Faith Ministries
    P.O. Box 748
    Chesterton, IN 46304

Printed in the United States of America

ISBN 13: 978-1-936270-51-4

For Alexa and Sophia
—J. H.

Contents

Acknowledgments

It is only appropriate that I include a few words of gratitude for those whose combined support made this work possible. I am, along with all those other believers who have been so deeply moved by Abba Matta's sermons, deeply indebted to the Monastery of St. Macarius for their diligence in recording every word possible that the spiritual master spoke and for joyfully blessing my efforts in this endeavor.

My sincere appreciation is also due to the publishing team at Ancient Faith Publishing, which graciously accepted to publish this book, perceiving the value of the spiritual ruminations of a great father of the Orthodox Church—though translated by one who possesses no considerable reputation. Katherine Hyde, always accessible and supportive, has been my go-to person in every respect.

I am indebted to my parents and my country, which provided me with the two languages involved in the preparation of this work. I thank my wife, whose loving support extends to every task which my hands and mind are set to accomplish. And I thank my God for each breath of life poured into me, and for His love, mercy, and hope.

Introduction

A dear friend of mine, much my senior, once related to me the
story of a trip he took with his Sunday school class during his
primary school years in Egypt. His teacher was Nazir Gayed—a
prominent figure in the Coptic Sunday school movement that
took place in the early twentieth century, who would eventually
be appointed the 117th Patriarch of the Coptic Church. Nazir had
promised the students an interview with an exceptional figure he had
encountered in recent years who had absorbed his entire admiration.

The class traveled to *Deir el-Suryan*, or the Monastery of the Syr-
ians, and waited expectantly for the notable person to arrive. Finally,
they began to discern the outline of someone approaching them from
the desert landscape. "Take a good look," said Nazir to his pupils.
"Many generations will come and go before the Church sees another
man like this."

The hermit came and sat with the little group. The spiritual
words that came out of his mouth (as my friend says it) were some
of the most beautiful thoughts they had ever heard. After the group's
interview with him, the hermit—who was Abba Matta—gave their
teacher a handwritten manuscript of his first pending book, *Orthodox*

Prayer Life, to which Nazir had the privilege of writing a short preface.

The following approximately forty years would see the unfolding of the most illustrious spiritual, literary, and monastic career of recent memory in the Coptic Church. In the Christian world of Egypt, it is virtually impossible to avoid the influence exerted by Fr. Matta's mind. One friend I met there told me that, after the thrill of reading his books, it was difficult for him to read anything else. Another told me he had listened to one of Fr. Matta's recorded messages on the Holy Spirit thirty times, and he still couldn't get to the bottom of it. Another dear acquaintance of mine, a Protestant minister, frequently (and subtly) weaves Fr. Matta's ideas into his own sermons.

We in the New World are just beginning to develop an awareness of this unique historical personage from the East. Some might suggest that we have saints enough from both East and West, and the literature they have left behind already overwhelms us. But Abba Matta's teaching does not simply increase an already swollen flood of books. He has a new perspective to offer our generation.

Why do we need a new perspective? With the rolling on of days and the forward movement of a wearisome life, faith and zeal tend to fall into a slumber. People can easily get discouraged with spiritual life—it needs to be constantly aroused and revitalized by the witness of some contemporary saint, some man or woman whom God raises up for the very purpose of leading a prophetic life. We need these spiritual pioneers to exhort us to keep up the fight; we need what in the Old Testament were called the "prophets." They are God's agents sent into the world to rekindle a dying faith.

Father Matthew the Poor was eminently one of these spiritual pioneers. His teachings breathe new life into an Orthodoxy that is constantly at risk of growing stiff due to the incessant heaping up of rubrics and formulae. To stand at attention during the Divine Liturgy is one thing; to bring the spiritual fruits of prayer and worship into one's everyday world is another. To recite the Creed is one thing; to live a life of genuine faith and love in Father, Son, and Holy Spirit is quite another. Abba Matta's difficult task was, firstly, to find joy in the deeper meanings of the traditions and doctrines that shape our Orthodox belief; and, secondly, to expound and communicate that joy for the profit of other believers.

But, I have often wondered, why can't we all experience this revitalization of faith simply by reading Scripture? Shouldn't the reading of God's Word produce in us a spiritual effervescence which no worldly power could ever quench? Yes, it should. But it is our over-familiarity with God's Word that has bred in us an idle indifference to the astonishing events and doctrines contained in Holy Writ. We may read, "Then Pilate took Jesus and scourged Him," without raising an eyebrow; but when we watch the shocking dramatization of that clause in Mel Gibson's film *The Passion of the Christ*, we shudder and weep.

The fact of the matter is that the Bible, the Church, and Christianity are all earth-shattering phenomena; but we live on in a stupor. Nothing moves us anymore; miracles do not surprise us; the Sermon on the Mount does not invigorate us; the Psalms do not strike us with awe. The ceaseless progress of technology has caused us to grow us accustomed to "wonders" without feeling grateful for them. Is it any surprise, then, that the Faith we hold is not producing many saints?

As an antidote to this widespread lethargy, Abba Matta's words effectively remind us of the soaring heights of joy and spirituality to which a strong faith can raise us. And he doesn't mince words. When he says things like, "Christianity is not designed for your pleasures. Either suffer through it and give thanks, or else return to the world," we feel we are listening to someone who has indeed touched the core of truth. When we read his Bible commentaries, we feel the power of Christian life return to the sacred page. When we reflect on that inspiring life, we feel convinced once again that prayer does indeed make a difference; that miracles do happen to the soul that believes; and that sacrifice of the self is the greatest good in life.

In one of his discourses, he says, "If there is a man who bears the dying of Christ, his life's story can never die and become extinct: rather, it will break out and expand and produce new saints. His life's walk will resuscitate others' souls, will awaken others' consciences, and will renew the lives of other people who were on the road to death. These are the lives of the saints which I am always urging you to read." In referring to the lives of the saints, he was unwittingly pointing to his own journey as well.

The mention of Abba Matta's life calls to my memory of couple of incidents which I would like to describe here for the sake of illustration. It is related that when Abba Matta was still a young pharmacist working in an area near Mt. Sinai, a few of his colleagues came to him with the proposal to visit St. Catherine's Monastery, situated some distance up the mountain nearby. Dr. Youssef, as Abba Matta was then called, initially refused to go, because he had made a commitment not to visit any monastery from that day forward except the one in which he would be received as a monk. But his friends pressed on him with constant entreaties until he finally yielded to their will and went along.

Dr. Youssef sat next to the driver of the car as they went up the mountain, and they came to a point where they began to drive over unpaved terrain because the road had ended. As they ascended higher and higher up the mountain, the darkness became thicker and blacker, and Dr. Youssef began to feel a trace of uneasiness steal into his body. The uneasiness quickly turned into a panic; his heart began to beat violently, and his airway closed up so that he felt a choking sensation. He turned and yelled at the driver to stop.

The car screeched to a halt, and Dr. Youssef stepped out of the car to take some deep breaths of the cool mountain air in order to regain his composure. He walked to the front of the car and noticed strong winds sweeping right before him. As he strained his eyes, he was shocked to realize that the direction they were heading led to a sudden drop only a few meters ahead of where they had stopped. They were, in fact, only seconds away from driving over a cliff. His friends were astonished at God's direct intervention in their lives and at the fine spiritual sense their friend Youssef then possessed.

Another story well illustrates the intimate connection between Abba Matta and his God. One day, during his years as abbot of the Monastery of St. Macarius, he developed conjunctivitis, a painful condition that involves redness and inflammation of the eyelid and inner tissue. Abba Luke, the monastery's medic and a former physician, had attempted to treat Abba Matta's condition with an Egyptian-made ointment, but it only intensified the inflammation and burning; so Abba Luke resorted to applying a European-brand ointment that was effective in reducing the symptoms and providing Abba Matta with some relief.

During treatment, Abba Luke informed Abba Matta that one of the workers in the monastery[1] had come down with a similar case of conjunctivitis but was being treated with the Egyptian-made ointment. Abba Matta ordered him to treat the worker with the European brand. Abba Luke objected that they had but one tube left, and since it was so difficult to obtain another tube of the same type, it clearly should be reserved for the monastery's abbot. Abba Matta responded, "You *must* go give it to our brother the worker." Abba Luke complied and took it immediately. It must be understood that Abba Matta was

---

1   The amount of labor needed to rebuild and maintain the vast monastery was beyond the capabilities of the monks who resided there; so the monastery employed a steady team of workers who streamed in from around the country to perform the physical labor in return for a reasonable stipend.

often reckless in his faith and occasionally did "unreasonable" things with the assumption that God was watching and would work things out, even if it endangered his own health, or in this case, his eyesight.

That very evening, the monastery received a visitor from Lebanon who was an old friend of Abba Matta's but whom he hadn't seen for many years. The visitor requested an interview with the abbot, but the monks responded that he wasn't meeting with anybody presently because he was ill. The visitor left a package, saying, "Please give this to Abba Matta; it's something he requested from me several years ago, but unfortunately I hadn't the chance to come pay him a visit until today. And give him my sincere regards." The monks brought the package to Abba Matta, and when he opened it, he found four full tubes of the same European-brand ointment he had sent to the worker. He went directly to his cell and offered up prayers of thanksgiving to God, "in a state of fire and tears," as he related, saying, "Oh, how faithful You are, O God!" The first reading of this story brought tears to my eyes as well.

Such was the man; such was his faith; and such was that rare and turbulent life of which the world has yet to hear the full details. The lives of most contemporary Orthodox saints have been elucidated to the fullest extent possible; but that of Abba Matta still lies largely in obscurity, and, like the ancient monuments of Egypt, will require years of research and excavation to bring into full light.

But one cannot justly praise the man in isolation from his surroundings. For just like those ancient monuments, Abba Matta was heavily indebted to the land and people in which he was formed. He was, indeed, a branch on a much greater tree called Coptic Christianity; and he did, like Sir Isaac Newton, "stand on the shoulders of giants." He learned monasticism from Anthony; Macarius taught him contemplative life; Pachomius taught him coenobitic life; Isaac of Nineveh taught him ascetic life; Athanasius and Cyril taught him theology; Mina the Solitary and Theophilus el-Suryani were his living directors; Dr. Aziz Atiya[2] was his portal of access to patristic literature.

His generous heart also took in all the learning he could get from non-Egyptian sources: Basil, Gregory the Theologian, and John Cassian were some of his favorite church fathers, and he studied modern exegetes like Lightfoot and Wescott to learn what the finest modern scholarship of the Bible had to say. As John Donne wrote, "no man is an island" in spiritual life; and Abba Matta was fully conscious of the debt he owed to the spiritual masters who went before him.

We send up a prayer that in reading Abba Matta's words, the reader might feel the same congenial showers of delight fall upon his or her soul which long ago fell upon the soul of this translator, and made him glad.

James Helmy, translator
Feast of the Apostles, 2015

---

2   Founder of the Institute of Coptic Studies in Cairo during the 1950s, and founder of the Middle East Center at the University of Utah, in addition to a host of other positions and chairs held at various academies throughout the course of his career. The first set of the Nicene and Post-Nicene Fathers library ever to make it into Egypt was sent by him as a gift to Abba Matta.

Faith in the Impossible[1]

1981

ON CHRISTIAN SERVICE

One of the major problems with service in the Church today is that the servant wants to rejoice in his service before Christ does. He yearns to see a profit before Christ sees it. He wants to enjoy the strength and gladness that return to him from his ministry and to use the incoming fruits as a stimulus for further service.

We must, however, understand a basic principle of our ministry: that this ministry is not our own. Whatever we say of our service is only derivative. When we speak of "our ministry" or "our children," we are really speaking of Christ's ministry and Christ's children. A priest will often say, "Pray for me. My ministry is weakening and my flock is weary." No, father priest, wake up and realize that it is Christ's own

---

1   This chapter is a dialogue Abba Matta had with some visitors to the monastery. The first part includes some of his comments regarding Christian service, and the second part includes his remarks on faith in the impossible.

ministry, and it is His flock—you are one of the sheep—and He is the only Shepherd. I must indeed personally befriend the children I serve, but He is the true Friend. I am only carrying out my steward-ship for their service, and I must one day give an account of my stew-ardship to my Master. It is the Master alone who has the authority to tell me, "Well done, good and faithful servant."

So our understanding of service needs to change. Only the Lord possesses a perfect awareness of His flock's needs. Only He can decide when to grow it, when to shrink it; when to fuel it with zeal, and when to compassionately tend it because of its weakness; when to require hard labor of it, and when to give it rest. That's His job. My job is simply to stand at a distance to perceive His will and to follow His leading.

I cannot consider myself ultimately responsible for the amount of fruit His ministry produces. It is very possible that He wants to use my name for His service but not my fruit. He might want to serve through my lowliness but not through my words. Some people have been edified simply by my abjectness when I had nothing profitable to say. What kind of "fruit" are we to look for otherwise? In the past I've been told, "We like you"; but that still leaves doubts in my mind. Did what I told them benefit them? Was their praise mere words? It has often seemed to me that my words yield a very small advantage to the hearers. I have often felt that my efforts go unrewarded.

But a servant ought not to think like this. Your efforts might be completely successful; they could be making those you serve better than you and more worthy of eternal life. Do you think your job is to make everyone a scholar like yourself? Or to stuff them with knowl-edge like yourself? They may have found a door to salvation you don't know about; it's a small and lowly door, which you have to empty yourself of all your accolades and degrees in order to fit through.

Sometimes God serves (unknowingly to us) through our

reputation in other places. For example, a person might be serving in a church in Shubra,[2] and his ministry affects people in Alexandria;[3] but the people he serves in Shubra pay him no attention. He will be tempted to murmur and say, "Why are all the churches around me filled with people while my church is empty? Don't I serve just as well as the servants in other churches?" As he grows old, he complains to God, "Why didn't I reap the benefits of my toil?" And approaching death, he says, "All have forsaken me,[4] and I am alone. Woe is me, and woe is my ministry! Everyone else has achieved success but me. I must have been serving in the wrong field. Those whom I served proved to be unworthy of my words and my service. Oh, my ministry was such a waste!"

Who said such things? St. Paul did. But Paul died, and dioceses sprouted up everywhere afterwards. God served the world through Paul's name and through Paul's death, and the fruit reaped thereby has been many, many times more valuable than the fruit reaped during Paul's life. His death proved to be a hundred thousand times more productive than his life.

Our service, you see, cannot be weighed or evaluated by the level of our exertions. Neither can our service be weighed by the number of people who follow us or listen to our sermons. Christian ministry should never be gauged by size or by numbers. I will tell you by what Christian ministry should be measured: our willingness to die to the world. If you have truly died to the world and taken Christ into your heart, be certain that your service can never fail, but will rather continue to shine from generation to generation.

---

2   Famous city in Egypt with a high concentration of Christians and churches.
3   Alexandria is about 150 miles north of Shubra.
4   2 Tim. 1:15

FAITH IN THE IMPOSSIBLE

If you act based solely on your natural capabilities, you will never achieve very much. For example, you wake up one Sunday sick, weak, cold, and unable to travel to church. The devil comes and reasons with you: "Look, you're in very bad shape today. Poor thing! Today is just not the day for church. Stay home and sleep."

Your ability to attend church that day is only ten percent. But that one out of ten chance is not a minor thing! You can start with it. You decide to get dressed and go to church. You arrive and happen to run into someone very important to you, and thus one of the great sagas of your life begins. "Strange thing," you say. The little work you did grew and multiplied and produced a hundredfold.

We do not have more than a ten percent ability to believe and trust in God's words. For example, you go to do a certain work, and you are not convinced that it will succeed. "But in the name of Christ, I will *begin*." You will be amazed at the power that enters you, at the paths that open up, at the grace that fills your life, and at the diligence and youthfulness that inspire your body to do that work you were so hesitant and afraid to start. The grace that changed everything continues with you five, ten, or fifty years; and you proceed to talk about it the rest of your life. The story of God's work in any saint's life is a marvelous and amazing story; and it begins with the impossible.

When I first decided to enter monasticism,[5] there was not a human being who met me without telling me that I was out of my mind. Monks, bishops, priests, friends, family—they all said I was crazy. It was because monasticism at the time was a dead enterprise. No one

---

5   The following few remarks are the response to a question posed by someone in the audience. The question revolved around the faith needed to complete the monumental feat of rebuilding and reviving the Monastery of St. Macarius, and whether Abba Matta had really expected beforehand all to happen that had happened.

was going that way. And the monks then living were not really prac-ticing on the level of true monasticism. Many of them joined monas-ticism for the wrong reasons; for example, many had caused some major trouble in the world, and they entered the monastery to flee from their problems.

Maybe some of you know the story of Havez Nagib. He became a monk in one of the monasteries, was ordained a priest, then an arch-priest. In reality, he was a Muslim and one of the largest crime-leaders in Egypt. So he acted the part of a priest, writing, preaching, and even praying liturgies. He was eventually nominated to become the Metro-politan of Ethiopia. So he went to meet Patriarch Kyrillos VI,[6] a man of keen spiritual vision, accompanied by an entourage of supporters who had gone to recommend him to the Patriarch.

"All right, bring in that blessed man of yours," said the Patriarch. Nagib stepped forward. "Is that you, Nagib, who has produced this wicked deceit? Ah, may God have mercy on the Church because of you!" Nagib says that he was about to black out and faint. He returned to the monastery, threw off his robes, and fled. These details are all recorded in a book he wrote about his personal confessions.

So that was the quality of monasticism during the days we left the world to join them, when we were without health, or strength, or a friend to encourage us, but only warnings from everyone about how this way would lead to death. But I was going out with trust in the story of my ancestors, that is, in the history of the Church, and in the story of the monks and saints whom we commemorate at the altar. Either that story was true (so I told myself), and monasticism was real, or else the whole Church was wrong and the Bible itself a mistake. Why couldn't I test these things for myself and live them? I desired to live for God, so why shouldn't I?

I went out with my chances of success being one out of ten. The

---

6   The longest-sitting Patriarch of Alexandria, 1874–1927.

result was that I suffered considerable pain. I have been a monk now for thirty-four years; and though I've experienced immense hardship, the amount of good I've profited from the monastic life is far beyond what I could have profited in any other lifestyle. What I've gained from the Old and New Testaments, from the Church's history and theology, from inward faith, from my relationship with Christ, and from my love for God could not have been gained in any other way. Sometimes people ask, "If you were given a second chance at life, would you become a monk again?" I answer with an absolute yes. Yes: in the same way, and in the same place! Because the things that cost me so much hardship are precisely what built up my faith and moved me forward in spiritual life.

"Well then, what are the principles that have steered your life?" They are these: faith in the impossible and faith in the inconceivable. When I first entered monasticism, I was not physically or mentally fit to be a monk. My spiritual faculties were very weak. I was like any young man living in the world; I hadn't read the Bible through, but I did love God. The principle that moved me forward (and which I still profess today) is that if a person desires to have faith in Christ, he must resolve in his heart to believe in the impossible. You can apply this in the intellectual or natural life as well, and it will sometimes work. But when applied through Christ, it works one hundred percent. People say that self-confidence and determination cause a person to succeed. This may be true, but not absolutely so; in Christ, however, it is absolutely true. If our belief in the Christian faith and our belief in God's promises are merely up to the level of what is conceivable to the human mind, we will never build something great upon such a basis.

The cumulative experience of God's children and God's saints points to a life based on doing the impossible. Think of any saint, even the worst of them. Two renowned saints were the vilest of men:

Augustine and Moses the Black. Augustine had led a bad life and was drowning in sin. His mother continually wept for him; so she went to a good bishop by the name of Ambrose and requested his prayers. He told her, "The son of such abundant tears can never be lost. He will one day return to God. Do not be afraid." Today, Augustine is called the Prince of Mysticism, and he has become the greatest of Christian philosophers.

Moses the Black was a depraved criminal, a murderer, and led an extremely debased life. He could eat an entire lamb at one sitting. He was once standing on the banks of the Nile and saw a flock of sheep on the other side. So he decided to cross the river with the intention of murdering the shepherd and stealing the sheep. Once night fell, he took his knife between his teeth and began swimming. In the middle of the way, God's voice came to him and said, "Moses, haven't you done enough? Haven't you ruined enough people already?" He became dejected and swam back to the river bank. He sat on the ground forlorn as the voice pounded in his head, saying, "Repent!" Thereupon he went to one of the monasteries and told them, "I would like to repent." This was coming from a gigantic, frightful man. It was said that, after he became a monk, ten thieves once invaded the monastery to plunder it. Moses the Black tied them all with a rope and dragged them to the monks. This man, by the power of repentance latent in him, became a patron saint of the Paromeos Monastery. How many other such stories there are in the annals of the Church!

Let us also take the case of a famous woman—that there be neither male nor female in Christ Jesus.[7] She had been walking the streets of Alexandria, corrupting many of the young men, until she decided to travel to Jerusalem, seeing there greater opportunities for her dissolute lifestyle. She happened to pass by the Church of the Resurrection and was confronted by the icon of St. Mary. She saw

---

7   Gal. 3:28

the face smile at her, and she stood in a daze. The smile seemed to say to her, "Enough!" Her heart was captivated. That very moment she turned around, went and changed her clothes, and began to enquire how she could start a life of repentance. She straightway went to the Jordan wilderness, hid herself in the hidden depths of that desert, and there lived for over twenty years. She saw not a single person all that time, and she would cover her body with whatever material she found at hand.

One day, the saint and priest Zosimas spotted her in the desert, and thinking she was some form of animal, followed her. She suddenly turned around and said, "Stop; I am a woman." Fear seized him; and standing a long distance away from her, he asked her who she was. She said, "I have left the world. I used to live in Alexandria, but I came here to repent and to live for Christ. I would like to receive communion." He replied, "Well. Remain where you are." He obtained the eucharistic elements from Jerusalem and returned to offer them to her. She said, "I would like to partake again after a period." He went to obtain the eucharist again, and when he returned—this part affects me deeply[8] . . . he found her dead. Next to her in the sand were written the words, "From dust unto dust."[9]

These days parents shudder at the idea of their son or daughter leading the monastic life. "How can they live in the desert or the mountains? What a deprived life!" As if *we* are deprived of something. Some people come and say, "You monks sometimes take things a little too far. On the outside your desert life is quaint, but on the inside there is just too much asceticism. No meat; no eggs; no sweets; vigils; sleeping on the ground. It's just too much." But what do you think of Mary of Egypt and her life in the mountains? Palestine during the

---

8   There is an audible quiver in Abba Matta's voice at this point, followed by a short silence, showing the deep emotional impression the story has made on him.

9   Gen. 3:19

winter is a freezing wilderness, and she was an Alexandrian, accustomed to the warm Egyptian climate.

The whole of Russia has taken Mary the Ascetic as its patron saint; and there is a church to Mary the Ascetic in France. The whole story of her life is a picture of the impossible. She was a lonely woman wandering in the inner desert. From the world's point of view, her actions were complete insanity. But if you were to ask her what she was doing, she would have said, "I'm going to live for God."

"What God are you talking about? Our God is beyond human reason, and you're just a woman."

"Let me be. I know where I am going. He will overshadow me."

How did she survive in the desert? I will tell you: God's direct protection. It surrounded her and shielded her from the wild beasts—which came rather to lick her wounds—from thieves, from heat, and from natural hazards.

I had a small taste of such things. When I suffered severe lack of food, my body was still somehow satisfied. When the cold grew brutally severe, and my circulation slowed down, I still felt warmth. There were times when I had neither food nor clothing nor medicine, and survival seemed all but impossible. There was one particularly hard winter that came at a time when I had nothing to wear except a short-sleeved shirt. The cold froze my head and limbs, and my brain was so numb I could not think. But then, by faith, I gradually began to feel as though I were standing in the sun with a full stomach. The sensation made me tremble with fear, because I felt at that point that something beyond the normal had entered me. But very shortly afterward, God sent me clothing, because I didn't have enough faith to sustain me in that type of life forever. The point I want to make is this: The potential power of an intense faith can achieve things inconceivable to the mind.

✛ ✛ ✛

What is a miracle? It's the product of faith *without* the logical mind. Faith *with* logic cannot produce miracles. For example, a man has a terminal illness, and the doctors tell him there's no treatment. He says to the priest, "Pray for me, Father; maybe God will allow a miracle." But he says this neither believing in what he says nor waiting for the miracle to happen. And it doesn't.

Then there is a mother whose child has a terminal illness, who believes, but whose friends tell her to stop crying, because the doctors have spoken the sentence and it's all over. But her answer is, "God is rich in power." They say, "The doctors have already said the disease is too firmly established in the body. And anyway, the era of miracles belongs to the past." The mother, however, does not cease to weep and to trust in God.

One woman had a husband who suffered a terrible fracture in his leg, and the doctors told him it would never be healed. He consulted the best doctors in Egypt and England, but they told him he was too old for proper healing, and he would limp and hobble about the rest of his life with a cane. But the wife continued to weep, pray, and insist on a miracle. She came here to tell me that she expected a miracle to happen. I encouraged her and urged her to persist in faith. (Her faith was indeed very strong.) Miracle after miracle began to occur, until one day her husband threw away his cane. He began to walk independently, and quite swiftly, too. God gave her precisely what she desired.

These are not mere fantasies or stories from the early Church. These are wonders performed today in the name of Jesus and by the power of the Gospel. The Gospel's power cannot be grasped by the logical mind. A man may come to me and say, "I'm a sinner." I answer him, "Then God loves you tremendously, for He loves sinners. He came down from heaven specifically for sinners. Do not be afraid. Love Him. If you love Him, your conscience will never trouble you about the things you did in your past."

He replies, "Abba, I need a very long time to repent of the things I've done." But I persist in showing him God's love. He returns one day and says, "Abba, the miracle has happened! I felt the love of Christ of which you spoke. I feel as if I've been born once again and made into a new creature." The man grows jubilant and goes out to tell others about holiness, repentance, and life with Christ. The greatest preachers ever to have lived, who brought the most souls to salvation, were originally the worst of men. They *tasted* God's ability to sanctify their lives and to cleanse their consciences.

What is the amount of your faith in Christ? How much does your trust in Him defy logic? As long as your faith uses logic as a prop, it will continue to crawl along the floor like an infant. It will never stand on its own two feet. The day a person says, "How long will I continue to doubt God's work in my life? How long will I doubt God's ability to raise me up on my feet, as it is written in the Bible, and grant me all the rights and blessings of the saints? I will start to trust God completely"—once he says that, he will immediately begin to feel the Spirit moving within him. He will feel divine love enter his heart and heat it up.

And at that point he begins to feel something of a separation forming between himself and the world. No longer will everything that takes place in the world reverberate inside him. No longer will all the world's events affect him. He starts to have a sense of discernment, an ability to know the difference between those things that deserve his attention and those that do not. There are things in the world that warrant our concern—like our children or our career—but the concern is felt through the lens of complete trust in Christ. I have concern over certain things with the assumption and belief that God will provide every solution.

But there are some things about which we ought *never* to worry. For example, when someone threatens your life. Do not let it cause you one ounce of anxiety! If someone says to me, "I will kill you," I respond, "Well, then what's taking so long?"

A private detective once came to me (this was back in 1955), saying, "We have received a letter detailing a murder threat against you, and I'm ready to protect you."

I told him, "Look, your honor, I need to explain something. Do you know what I would say to someone approaching me to kill me?"

"What?" he asked.

"I would open my outer tunic and tell him, 'Strike me right here.' Now, if you would like me to pray for God's protection *over you*, I'm prepared to do it. But you will never be able to protect me."

There are things that are just not worth suffering anxiety over. I was once living in a desolate cave in the mountains, where the devil would periodically come to me with frightening intimations, saying, for example, "The wolves will be coming to you hungry today, and they will gnaw at your flesh." And at night, I would hear the wolves howling very near my cave. My nerves would twitch as the wolves came closer and closer and finally lay down at the door of the cave. They would come in a pack of two or three; that is, with the direct purpose of attacking me.

This trial occurred on the very first night of my time in the mountains. I prayed, "What is this, Lord? Isn't the God of these wolves the same God as Yourself? Can these wolves come inside without You allowing them to do so?" So I went and fetched a cup of water and prayed over it; then I went to the door, kicked it open, and sprayed the water on the wolves. They immediately fled. I was overjoyed! I closed the door and went to sleep. They didn't appear the following night. Afterwards they developed the habit of coming to my door every night and scratching and knocking at it. But the danger was past.

There are things, as I said, that do not deserve our anxiety. "My income is not enough." Do not worry over it. "People are threatening my employment at work." Do not be anxious about it. Hold your head high, for you are not merely working under an unfair boss, but rather under Christ Jesus, who can shake heaven and earth for your sake. By such an attitude we can live in a world filled with pain, want, and threats. We must have a mind capable of discerning between matters worthy of our anxiety as children of God—that is, the problems of *others*—and matters unworthy of anxiety, that is, things that concern *ourselves*. And there are some things that can never merit our worry at all.

This attitude is supported by our faith in the impossible. This is also illustrated by the example I commonly use of the woman standing on the third floor of a burning building, who sees Christ standing on the ground and feels confident in jumping. But if she sees a mere human standing below, telling her to jump, she'll refuse. "I'd prefer to be consumed by the fire than to jump." But if it were Christ standing below, she would be more than eager to jump. Know that the most pleasing thing there is to Christ is the opportunity to reveal His power to His children. "My strength is made perfect in weakness."[11] His power is not made perfect in the strong, but in the weak.

I want to conclude this discussion with a few final thoughts. This generation of youth in our country and the world lacks ears to hear. A father comes to his son and tells him, "My son, I want to give you a piece of advice, which is really the inheritance of a lifetime. When someone does you a wrong turn, do not retaliate."

"What do you mean, father? Should we live like cowards?"

"My son, I am telling you something that will benefit you in life."

"No, father, that type of thinking applied to your past generation. I'm from the new generation that takes the bull by the horns." It's a generation that refuses to hear the counsel of its elders. How will it listen to the counsel of the Bible?

---

11   2 Cor. 12:9

The advice of parents is at least supported by logic: "Son, you must study in order to succeed." But the Bible does not talk like that. The Bible tells him to trust in Christ, and he will be lifted above every fear on earth. It promises to give him things beyond anything he could imagine. I am hesitant to say it, but this pertains even to material things. If you don't have enough money, but you do have plenty of trust in God, He will support your work. If you have large amounts of material to study, but insufficient time to cover it all, you must trust in God! Don't you love Christ? Don't you pray? Have you done your part? Then you will make it.

I once went through this with a young man, and it changed his life. He had become so worried that he was on the verge of losing his mind. The problem was that he had spent most of his days in medical school playing around, and now his education was in jeopardy. The educational demands became so heavy on him that he began to weep.

There was a natural familiarity between us because we are relatives, so he came straight to me. "What are you crying about?" I asked. He replied, "I'm failing the year." He had missed most of his lectures, neglected his studies, and was now in danger of repeating the entire year. He was in a state of sore depression. He told me, "Just pray for me, because the year is lost. I won't even sit for the final exam."

It occurred to me that taking the exam and failing the year would provide him with better experience than not taking it at all; so I said, "No, go and sit for it." That's the reasoning I initially used to push him into it.

He said, "I haven't attended any of the lectures."

I said, "But I will pray for you."

"So you think I may pass?"

"Well, why not?" was my reply.

"Are you being serious or joking?"

"Absolutely serious."

"So there's a possibility of making it?"

"I believe so."

"But I haven't studied a thing."

"Well, but there is a God, and He is a resource we can trust in to compensate for our losses, our ignorance, and our sin."

I sensed in him a willingness to act. I continued, "If you want this to work, go and get the lecture notes for the entire previous year, and sit and read them over. You have one month. Just make sure you read them in a calm state of mind. Then go take the exam."

"And I'll pass?"

I said, "You will pass."

He said, "Listen. If I don't pass, I'll make you look real bad!"[12]

I considered that this kid had potential for faith and for a real life with God. He had an excellent character; he had just drifted away from God, from the Bible, from confession, from everything spiritual. It was quite a mess. But he trusted me, so he came requesting my prayers. I felt as though he were testing my own faith, and I told myself, "Will my faith lose to a person like this?"[13] God knows it was a real trial of both our faith. So every so often I would call him and ask if he were doing his studies. I would tell him in the most tranquil tone of voice, "Simply read. If you particularly like a certain passage, read it again. And make sure you read all the lectures."

When the results were posted, he was so scared to see his score that he stayed home. He normally had nerves of steel, but this particular thing terrified him. He received a phone call from an acquaintance telling him he had passed! He scolded the caller, telling him he was a liar and accusing him of playing jokes on him.[14] The caller responded,

---

12 General laughter from the audience.
13 Again, general laughter.
14 Laughter.

"Just come and see the list!" He half-dressed himself and ran like a madman to see the score posted next to his name. He then came here half-crazed, yelling out, "I believe in God! I believe in God!"[15]

Christ does not intend just to hear our pious prayers and worship; but He intends to intervene in our schooling, our fights with others, our problems with the government, our problems at work, and everything else. He is the great architect and builder of our lives—in the little things just as much as in the big.

✟ ✟ ✟

"Lord, I believe. Help my unbelief!" Very good.[16] This means, "Lord, my faith rates a one out of ten. Will you accept it?" He *will* accept it. He needs something to work with. If there is no faith at all, He has nothing to work with. We have the case of Nazareth: "He could do no mighty work there . . . and He marveled because of their unbelief."[17] And as a contrast we have blind Bartimaeus.[18] The people tried to silence him, but he cried out even louder. "Who is yelling?" "It's just a blind man who wants to be healed." "Then bring him here." They brought him. "What do you desire?" "I desire to be healed." "Do you believe?" "I believe!" He received his sight. Why did Christ do that? He performed this miracle to give *us* new eyes. Bartimaeus eventually died, and his eyes were eaten by worms; but Christ is telling us that He can renew our vision and give us new life.

The critical question is this: "Do you believe?" This is Christ's question to the world. "I can do all things. I can bring peace. I can destroy the weapons of the enemy. *Do you believe?*" But we refuse to believe.

15 Laughter.
16 Abba Matta now responds to a question regarding the meaning of the phrase, "Lord, strengthen my faith."
17 Mark 6:5, 6
18 Mark 10:46, 47

Very unfortunately, we do not have the level of faith needed for Christ to do all things. We have stopped Christ from doing what He desires to do with us. And we have specifically stopped Christ from working *in the Church* what He wishes. When the Church strays from her Christ, can He still function? He cannot.

We have indeed strayed from Christ. But He is willing and able to reform the Church and to fortify her against all dangers. God's hand is great and powerful, and we should have trusted completely in it from the very beginning! We are subjects of the King of Peace, who can restore to us our peace at the needed time. We should be following His guiding hand with all our hearts!

It's my hope that our youth have ears to hear—to hear the words of the wise in each generation, and to hear the words of the Gospel. The youth represent the vitality and strength of the Church. The Holy Spirit works powerfully in the young. If the Church is weak today, it is because her young are weak in spirit. But when the young are strengthened in spirit, and their faith is strengthened in Christ, the Church becomes reenergized. My plea to Christ is that He grant an active zeal to the people, the priests, and the bishops to proclaim that same Gospel our grandfathers and ancestors proclaimed. There is nothing to fear. God is near us.

How the Bible Changed My Life

1974

I became a monk in August of 1948. I went to a remote monastery called Deir Anba Samuel,[1] and I chose it because it had neither the reputation nor the conveniences that would stifle my monastic life. I arrived there and found merely three or four people, with no priest, nor money, nor anything else. And because of our deep poverty, a priest used to come only on feast days to pray the liturgy with us. These circumstances produced in me feelings of a deep and peaceful quiet.

What drew me out of the world was the Bible. The world had caused me great distraction from the Bible. I wanted to settle down and read it, to read it attentively and with good comprehension, but my job was devouring my life, from seven in the morning to eleven at night. I kept telling myself, "Well, maybe next year, or the year after . . ." but one year followed upon another, and the days of my life were all being spent away. I finally said to myself, "I can no longer suffer the world to defeat me; I *must* experience the full satisfaction of knowing Christ and His Word." I refused to let the world

---

1   The Monastery of St. Samuel the Confessor

steal my youth from me and claim the twenty-four hours of my days.

The first disclosure of my thoughts caused a storm. How could I do such a thing, they told me, when I still had duties and obligations to discharge in the world? I became despondent; and the more the duties multiplied, the more urgently did the feeling press upon me that I had to leave the world. My foremost desire in me was to offer Christ the twenty-four hours of my every day. So I took to praying, and struggling, and oh, how the bitter restraints still bound me! But God eventually freed me. Once I was freed, I delved straight into my Bible—which I still have till this day. I would read, and feel nourished, then read again, and be nourished again. My reading gradually increased till I was covering thirty, forty, and fifty chapters per day. It was a time of genuine consolation in the Word.

I began with the Book of Genesis, thoroughly contemplating to understand it well, and underlining in red the verses that spoke to me. (If you look into my Bible today, you'll find it all marked up in red.) I notated and highlighted every verse and story that I liked, and I read and reread all those parts until they entered in and became a part of my life. Then I went through Genesis again, jotting down notes on paper—and I used the only notebook and the only pen that were in the monastery, because there was almost no communication between the monastery and the outside world.

(I was actually pleased that I could not send or receive letters from anyone, because it meant the ultimate detachment from the world. My desire was not due to any psychological problem, not to hatred of the world or of people, but simply because I wanted to enjoy the Lord. As you all know, I love people. It's just that I wanted nothing and no one to dilute my love for Christ or to hinder my absorption of the Word. Even when I received a letter, I would take it next to a dim candle so that I couldn't see whose handwriting it was; I would pray over it, and pray for its sender, then surrender it to the flame.)

I reached a very high summit of joy, until a problem occurred to me that caused me grief to the point of tears. The Bible was really very large: the New Testament is a giant, and the Old Testament is another giant. I said, "Lord, I've begun my monastic life at the age of thirty; but I need the lifetime of Methuselah[2] to cover both testaments, their verses, their stories, even to enjoy every letter!" Once my mind opened up to the Bible, every word in it began to ring in my ears, and every verse had a sweet savor to me. So I began to weep, because I felt I could not live long enough to cover everything in the Bible, and I said to God, "Look, O Lord, I want to ask You for one of two things: either make my life exceedingly long, or else open the eyes of my understanding."

Well, to lengthen my life was not an easy thing. My digestion was weak, and the food of the monastery was a lamentable ordeal. The quality of the ingredients was quite poor, and the soup always thin. And whenever there was a luxurious item to be eaten, like cheese paste, we had to dilute it with enough water to be shared by all the monks. Such was the extent of our "nourishment." And of course, times of fasting were even harder. And so my body was very frail, and though I made an extended lifetime one of my requests to God, I knew it was unrealistic, because since I entered the monastery I had lost significant weight, and there were times when my breathing grew difficult. Then I said, "Lord, it seems that my life won't be very long. So what I ask You is to give me a quick spiritual understanding." The Lord has been kind to me for allowing me to persist from 1948 until today; but He has also given me spiritual perception. It is this that I would like to talk to you about today.

I told you how I began my life with the Bible. When I was still a secular, the tears never parted from me, because the world consumed every hour of my life, even every month and year. And I asked myself,

2   Biblical patriarch recorded in Genesis 5 who lived 969 years.

"What will I gain in the end from the world? Money?" But money was no longer an attraction to me; I began to abhor it. Money meant slavery. When it increased, it would seize me by the throat and demand that I work more to earn more. It would force me to run around more, to exhaust myself more, and I began to feel such a loathing for it because it subjected me to this tiresome servility. It would steal from me—no, not steal from me, but openly confiscate from me before my very eyes—my time and my life. I thus began to develop an allergy to money. So, as I was telling you, from the time I was in the world, I started to feel the absolute necessity of reading the Bible; and the reason I am still a monk today is my deep longing for the Bible.

I began to ask myself which path in life would allow me to be the most devoted to the Bible. I thought of entering the boating industry, working on ships and sailing the seas, because that way I would have abundant free time available to me. But no, that work would involve lots of toil and busyness and sickness; there would be no peace in that sphere. Again, I thought about becoming a camel-driver and working out in the deserts. My whole aim, you see, was to remove these regular clothes and to work out in a distant place where I could find some seclusion. Then I thought, why go to all this trouble? Why not go to the ultimate source of seclusion? Monasticism would be good for me! But my acquaintances tried to terrify me out of it; they said, "Don't you dare!" They vowed that monasteries were no place for the educated, and that there would be no position or role for me to take up there, and that I wouldn't be comfortable. I prayed, "Lord, the Fathers went into the desert and succeeded, and now they're in heaven. Please ease the path for your servant."

I even had a close friend whom I informed of my decision. At first he told me that monasticism is too tough and toilsome a thing, but I responded that I had fully made up my mind about the matter and there was no turning back.

Then he said, "You know what, then I'll join you!"

I said, "Do what you will; but as for me, I'm going."

He suggested that we speak with a certain bishop, a good and saintly man, who could tell us what to do. His name was Bishop Kyrillos the Ethiopian. I said, "Could any single person in the world tell us what's right to do? I told you that I'm going for certain."

My friend persisted in his pleadings until I finally agreed, and we went and found the bishop lying sick in bed. There was a short exchange between my friend and him, all the while he was lying facing the wall with his back to us. My friend then said, "I want to become a monk."

He replied, "A monk? Son, monasticism is a strenuous thing."

Then I said, "You see, Your Grace, I've given God a six-month deadline. If He does not send me out nicely, I'm going by force."

That's really what I told God. I said that if He didn't send me out easily, and relieve me of the problems and the restraints holding me back, then I would leave the world anyway, and let what may happen, happen! It was a dangerous stance to take. I had responsibilities and obligations to discharge, papers and contracts to finish, but I cared for none of this. "Six months, Lord!" I said. "If You release me, I will go in peace. If You don't release me, then I'll break myself free and go. I want to live for You."

So when I said this to the bishop, he turned around to face us and said, "What? What are you saying?"

I repeated the words. He said, "Do you solemnly swear this by God Himself?"

I said, "Yes."

He replied, "Son, you have faith. God will certainly send you out." Once I heard that, a fresh burst of faith entered me; this was even the testimony of a bishop, whereas I had never met a bishop before, because I had always lived the spiritual life out of the spotlight, in peaceful seclusion.

So I went out of the world with my face set resolutely toward my dream, which was the Bible. In the beginning, the Bible began to open itself to me little by little, and how happy I felt when I found Christ speaking to me through those words! He showed me my faults and my sins. I sensed that the words were pointed at me; and for the first time my life began to take shape. My mind took focus; my spirit awakened; and it dawned on me that my salvation and the rectification of my life, its renewal and empowerment, would only come by way of the Bible.

I took to praying profusely before reading the Bible, saying, "O Lord, this Bible was written for me, and it has lasted all this time—close to two thousand years—till I arrived and found it. I thank you, God, that you have brought the Bible all the way to me, and even in printed form! This Bible is *mine*. All of its books, beginning with Genesis, were written *for me*. Does it make sense that I die while having not read one of these books? No, Lord. I *must* read the entirety of both the New and Old Testaments. Abraham is my own father." Abraham is my father. Imagine a person lost and separated from his family, who after many years returns to them and reunites with his father, his uncle, his grandfather, and so on. What excitement! That was my experience: I was lost and separated from my family while in the world; then I came here and discovered them again.

So I made my way from book to book, and came to discover "the family of the household of God,"[3] who were my own family. I greeted each one and said "pleased to meet you," and "salutations to the household of God." These are the words of St. Paul; he says: "You, O Gentiles, were strangers from the people of Israel, who are the people of God, that is, the family of God." Israel was the firstborn, and the Gentiles were only strangers—and maybe even "dogs," if you remember

---

3   Eph. 2:19

the speech of the Canaanite woman.[4] So, up until the Cross, and until the blood shed upon it, we were aliens, without God and without hope in the world. But when Christ died on the Cross, He abolished the barrier that separated us from the Jews[5] and made us all one flock under one Shepherd. So he says, "Rejoice, O you Gentiles!" and by "Gentiles" he was speaking to your reverences. You are the household of God! So then, if you are members in God's family, then what is Abraham's relationship to you? Your father.

So, you see, reading the Bible shook me tremendously, and increased my longing, and revealed to me that I am not a stranger but a member of the household of God. I told myself that I was in need of knowing my family better. And oh, how I enjoyed those long nights spent in reveling in the Scriptures, reading through the events, and discovering my own place in them! There was the life of Abraham, his emigration, his journeys; there was Jacob and his servitude to Laban, the toil he exerted year after year, while I toiled alongside him the entire way. I cannot even begin to express to you—only Christ can—the significance of our calling to live out the "life" of the Bible in its entirety.

Ah, how delightful too was that forty-year sojourn in the desert! It is given to us to sojourn as well; because, as you know, if we do not pass through the desert of Sinai, we cannot inherit our Promised Land in heaven. If we do not know about the gifts and blessings that were given so generously to Israel in Canaan, neither will we know the heavenly blessings.

This is how I passed through the entire Bible, event by event, verse by verse, name by name—and found that it all belonged to me. I also found that I bore a personal relationship to each father and saint in the Bible, even were it only a small one, even if it were only the privilege of loosening his sandal-strap.

---

4   Matt. 15:26, 27
5   Eph. 2:11–14

I rejoice in this my inheritance, a vast and weighty one, which is the Word. Beloved, it's inappropriate for a monk to boast in anything, or else he would be unworthy of the habit he wears. But let me say this. When I was in the world, I never lacked money; it filled my pockets by the thousands. Whatever I wanted to buy, I bought, and whatever I wanted to possess, I possessed. But nothing could satisfy me; the only thing that could satisfy was God's Word. So after I had thought about it, I sold the world for the sake of the Word. Nothing is dearer to me than the Word. But does this mean that everyone who sells the world becomes a monk? Of course not. A man can be quite wealthy but still hold money in very light esteem; and the Word can be of more worth to him than all his assets combined, and the entire earth as well. Many of my own spiritual children are extremely wealthy, but their relationship to the Word is very powerful.

A WEALTHY FRIEND

There was once a man with a prominent name who had entered the faith only recently, who came to see who this "Matthew the Poor" was. When he arrived, the monks came and told me that so-and-so had come. I directed them to meet with him themselves, but they responded that he had come specifically to see me; so I went to him. When I approached him, he looked at me and found nothing impressive in my stature, or my face, or my appearance; and he seemed disappointed to have made such a long trip for nothing.

Anyway, he had brought with him an atheist friend. This atheist asked me a question, and what a question it was—you know these atheists can be very shrewd. When I heard the question, I straightened up, because it was an intensely profound one; it showed me the caliber of the person before me. I have a strong attraction to those who are distant from God, especially those atheists who have read the Bible and know what they are talking about.

I asked him, "Are you ready to listen?" He said, "Yes." "Do you have time?" "Yes." So I began the discourse with him, as his friend listened on, and delved into very deep quarters of thought, all along using his own logic and his own philosophy. From there I made my way into the Bible, and proceeded to press him with a multitude of verses, until he finally yielded. This atheist was a large, impressive figure to the other; but when his friend saw him yielding, the atheist's image began to shrink in his friend's eyes.

So he in turn decided to ask a question. He said, "I have heard about Christ; but I would like to form a relationship with Him. But how? When I read the Bible, I feel like a stranger to it. I feel like the words are not meant for me, and that Christ is not meant for me either, so I lose interest in the Bible. And I'll be quite honest with you, I'm living life on my own terms right now."

I responded, "It's simply a result of being far away from Christ. Once you draw near to Him, your life will correct itself." I began to share a few verses with him and to clarify them with a little explanation. His heart was shaken. He asked me to jot down a certain verse for him which he particularly liked, and I did.

He came back after fifteen days and said to me, "Look, what you said has made my head spin, and my life is miserable. I can neither live my own kind of life anymore, nor can I live the godly life. So I've come to receive your absolution and permission to live without the Bible and without Christ. I want to go back to living my own kind of life. I've come to receive your absolution because my conscience is bothering me."

I told him, "May God absolve you then, but only if you *can* go back to your old life. You appear to be already caught!"

"What do you mean?" he asked.

"God is my witness that my eyes can see these things. The Spirit has caught you, because you are a child of God. No matter how much you kick back, you won't get loose."

He said, "No! No, this path is not made for me, and I'm just not up to it."

I said, "Fine," and he left on that note.

He came back after ten to fifteen days, saying, "I'm having a very hard time. Please, show me the way!" I said, "I will, little by little." So we worked together little by little, and he started to find spirituality satisfying and fulfilling. He finally took hold of the Bible. Ah, beloved, he returned after another ten to fifteen days with a list of thirty to forty questions, and how powerful they were! They were all practical, just like the first one he had asked, on how one can develop a relationship with Christ. I picked out two or three of them and provided responses for them, and told him that it was enough for the day. He asked how to pursue the spiritual life thereafter. I said I wouldn't assign him any rule or exercise, but all he needed was for the Bible to bloom in his life. So he began on the spiritual path and grew warm in the spirit.

At that point, Satan mounted his attack—"Satan has asked to sift you"[6] —he grew weary, then became resentful of me and stopped coming. But his conscience stirred him again, and he again came back to me, saying, "I wanted to let you know that it's all over. I've gone back into Satan's bosom." I told him, "If you are truly able to find rest in Satan's bosom, then I say the Bible is false, and the devil is right. You're really in for it." He said, "Don't frighten me! It looks to me like you work for the devil himself!" I responded, "Not at all. God knows I'm working for you by the power of the Spirit."

He left again, then returned after a while, saying, "The sinful path

6   Luke 22:31

is not for me anymore. I'm done with it." So this rich man began fasting intensely, and reading the Bible exhaustively, and going of his own initiative to the books of the great Church Fathers. He began reading the works of Athanasius in great depth, underlining and annotating here and there, and striving to increase his understanding.

He finally came to me exhibiting totally new principles in life. He said, "See, Abba, my old life has come completely to an end. And I've learned this first of all: that without staging a manly resistance to the flesh, it is impossible to be saved."[7] God knows those were the actual words spoken at the discussion, and you may call any monk who was present as witness.

He continued, "Secondly, I've learned that sin, once it has entered a person's head and dominated the brain, moves downward to the lower parts of the body and controls a person's desires. Therefore, if a person does not begin at the level of thought, and imbibe the Word so that it enlightens the mind, it's virtually impossible to defeat sin." I responded, "Blessed be God."

He said, "I need some words from you now." I rejoined that there were no words to be said after that. I said, "But it seems you've embraced the ascetic life a bit too quickly. So much asceticism is meant for someone like me, a monk." He answered, "It doesn't matter whether one is a monk or a secular person. To make progress, a person must begin at the door of fasting and asceticism. And I don't mean by *fasting* merely refraining from certain foods and eating with oil. Rather, a person needs a period of complete abstinence." These are the results of his personal experiences, gleaned from only five or six months of toil.

Where did he get all this? From the *Word*. He has become an example in my life. My entire relationship with him was merely an

---

7   This statement provoked an audible murmur of approval from the audience.

alternating series of supports and threats. When he came with a good report, I supported him. When he came announcing his return to Satan, I said, "Farewell. See if you can handle it." This was not a monk secluded on a mountain; this was a rich man living in the world, with enough money to supply him with every pleasure and every sin available. But the Word illuminated the right path for him, guided him, and instructed him in the way of salvation. So it's not just about being a monk, or living in the mountains, or isolation. I'm telling you this story in order to relay my message more effectively.

FLUCTUATIONS IN THE SPIRITUAL LIFE

Our lives tend to oscillate between darkness and light. We swing between rising and falling, between truth and falsehood, between service and absence, between holiness and foulness, between honesty and deceit, between courage and cowardice—until we receive the Word, as a real, double-edged sword, and allow it to penetrate us and to divide unto the soul and spirit: "The word of God *is* living and powerful, and sharper than any two-edged sword, piercing even to the division of soul and spirit, and of joints and marrow, and is a discerner of the thoughts and intents of the heart. And there is no creature hidden from His sight, but all things are naked and open to the eyes of Him to whom we must give account."[8]

What is the meaning of these words? They mean, beloved, that man is composed of body, soul, and spirit. In the beginning of a person's life, when he is still a "natural" man, he fails to receive the things of God's Spirit. Spirituality is nonsense: "I don't have the patience for church, and, frankly, not for the Bible either. I can't stand your fasts and eating with oil and all that. Prayer is a waste of time." The soul

---

8   Heb. 4:12, 13. The audience recites the entire two verses, clause for
      clause, with Abba Matta.

of such a person is still unconscious. It has no awareness, no knowledge, and no understanding—like a newborn baby. All of its energies are invested in the flesh—food, drink, parties, entertainment, and the like. The *soul*,[9] in such a state, is caught between the flesh and the spirit. When the flesh is stronger than the spirit, the soul drifts toward it, and so it becomes a "fleshly" soul.

Let's contrast this with the spiritual man. You tell him, "Eat up!" He responds, "I've eaten, thank God." You say, "Well, eat more!" He says, "I'm content." You continue, "Look, these are new and exotic food delicacies, you must taste them." But he answers, "I'm fine, thank you," and reaches out only to pick from the most meager foods. During fasts, he's told, "Your health has been flagging lately; how about skipping the fast this year?" But he responds, "A man does not live by bread alone. Don't you believe? Health and strength come ultimately from God." In such a case, the spirit is stronger than the flesh, and so his is a "spiritual" soul.

The soul, when it follows after the flesh, becomes viler than the flesh itself. Why? Because the body can reach the point of satiety, where it's finally satisfied; but at that point the soul pushes it to eat even more, and it does, even to the point of vomiting. It's said that in the time of ancient Rome, if a person were invited to several feasts, and wanted to enjoy the meat at each separate party, he would intentionally regurgitate his meal between dinners. Is it the body that's doing this? Not at all; the body eats its fill and is content. The culprit is the soul (astonishing as it sounds, because it's not the soul itself that consumes the food), because its desires are harsher than the body's.

If we talk about the sins of vileness and impurity, we find that the body is again restrained within certain limits. You see a man going

---

9   In the following discussion, Abba Matta employs the word *soul* in the ancient Greek sense of the term (*psyche*), that is, the center of a person's will. The meaning is roughly coordinate with the modern concept of the "mind."

to the doctor and complaining that his sexual drive is deficient. The doctor asks, "Are you married?" "Yes." "Do you have any children?" "Ten." "And how often do you copulate with your wife?" "Oh, a long time ago, we would do it so often, but now I'm getting feeble, and I need you to give me something to enhance me." And the man making this request is over sixty years old. The fact is, the body has indulged in its pleasures quite enough and is satisfied. But what is *not* satisfied? The soul!

I want to show you to what an extent the soul can blind a person and injure his life. You see, beloved, when God created the body—think of these words: "O God the great and the eternal, who created man in *incorruption*"[10] —the body was created with certain natural drives by which it might live in health and fullness. It cannot be guided solely by the spirit, but needs its particular drives in order to live; and these bodily drives have natural limits. Now the soul must refrain from surpassing those limits, that is, from desiring things that exceed the body's natural drives. Take hunger, for example. It's a drive designed to make you eat, so that you may be filled and satisfied and give thanks. The danger comes when, after the body has satisfied its urges, the soul rises to exploit the drives and to force them to operate beyond their capabilities. The man takes to eating an inordinate amount and variety of foods, until his health fails and his strength collapses. I am saying these things to alert you to the danger of obsession with the pleasures of the flesh and the danger of surfeiting and pampering the body beyond its needs.

I want now to talk about our own condition. We are in the state in which the soul is at one moment heeding the flesh and at another heeding the spirit. Holy Week arrives; we perform a multitude of prostrations, we pray in a secluded corner of the church, we tell God

10 A famous line in the Prayer of Reconciliation from the Liturgy of St. Basil.

how much we desire to devote our lives to Him, and so forth. Then we go out into the world, we see the world's glamour and the world's wealth, and we adopt the world's anxieties, until the Word is silenced and Holy Week is forgotten. It is a perilous state of hypocrisy in which the soul exists: one moment in the world, the next moment in the spirit.

But here let us light up the path before us. The Word of God is living and active, sharper than any two-edged sword, which alone is capable—and not sermons or anything else in this world—of dividing between the soul and the spirit. It distinguishes between the spirit's work and the soul's work. O Lord, grant me spiritual insight, by Your Spirit, and grant them a nimble understanding, that we might realize the inestimable worth of Your Word.

A servant of God must read the Bible *devotedly*. I use the word *devotedly* so often because I like it. One must read devotedly, and pray devotedly, that the reading and prayer might bear fruit. But merely reading a half-hour in the morning and fifteen minutes at night— what they call "devotions"—is this the double-edged sword? I assume that a servant who lives that way, and who is complacent with himself for occupying an important place in the service, might pray before reading the Word and say, "Lord, let the sword divide between my soul and spirit, and show me my true self."

He will then meet the words, "Indeed you are called a Jew, and rest on the law, and make your boast in God, and know His will, and approve the things that are excellent, being instructed out of the law, and are confident that you yourself are a guide to the blind, a light to those who are in darkness, an instructor of the foolish, a teacher of babes, having the form of knowledge and truth in the law."

"Yes, that is me, Lord."

"You, therefore, who teach another, do you not teach yourself?"

"What's that now?"

"You who preach that a man should not steal, do you steal?"[11]

Ah, and then the teacher's mind wanders . . . the conscience reminds him of a recent situation in which he undoubtedly acted the thief. Such is this "teacher." What a shame. "Oh me! I teach people not to steal; and look, I steal. No, Lord!" He then lays the Bible down, and begins to weep.

What happened here? The Word became the *sword*. He fell on his face from the weight of his grief and wept, as though someone had really struck him with a sword. Beloved, those who have experienced this know what it's like. I myself have: a person feels the weight of his sins and asks how he could possibly live like that anymore; and how he could have the phony appearance of holiness; and how he could seem the teacher while he teaches the opposite of what he does.

He continues reading: "You who say, 'Do not commit adultery,' do you commit adultery?" What? He senses a finger pointing at him. And the Holy Spirit is behind it all. The message can be just a single verse, but the Spirit uses it to admonish him for three whole days. We read on: "You who abhor idols, do you rob temples?" Eh? What's that? This hits home especially with the priest. The ego may sometimes compliment a man who has reached a moderately high spiritual state. He enjoys the glory and honor he receives as he walks to and fro before the altar—but isn't this robbery of temples? It's stealing the glory of the temple's Owner! "No, Lord, find someone else besides me. My place is neither the teacher's seat nor the pulpit. Find me any mound of rubbish to sit on, Lord, that I might pursue my repentance."

Once a man came to me requesting to become a monk. He told me, "I will be your servant and sit at your feet, and so on and so forth." The dialogue was somewhat awkward, so I just remained silent. Later I found out that he went to the monks' common area, saying, "Only one or two years from now, I'll be made a priest, and you all will be

---

11   Rom. 2:17–21

kissing my hand!" I summoned him and told him that, if he really wished to enter monasticism, he needed to repent sincerely. So he did repent the right way, and later told me, "My greatest desire since childhood was that people should kiss my hand." Since they wouldn't ordain him in the world, he thought it easier to become a monk as a shortcut to priesthood. What lengths he would go to have people kiss his hand! Such is the deceit of the ego! When the ego takes command of a person, it wrecks his life. There are so many channels for self-deceit in life, especially in the area of religion and the ministry.

My beloved, I want to say once more that I have found such joyful fulfillment in God's Word. But this joy was not an affair of the mind; I don't want to be mistaken for a biblical scholar or some kind of interpreter or commentator. My joy in the Word is that it was to me a parent, a guide, an instructor, and a reliable physician. It has truly penetrated me like a sword and excised the cancers. The Word is living and powerful! If you receive it, you will be filled with grace upon grace. But if you live without it, you will ever live in blindness. Such is the strength of the Word in the Christian's life: "a lamp to my feet and a light to my path."[12] Never in my life have I found such a helper and guide as the Bible. One must bow one's head before it in utter submission, just as one bows before a celestial king.

---

12   Ps. 119:105

The New Man

1974

The Gospel[1] we read today, my beloved, is the hope of all mankind. The message of this passage speaks with the utmost clarity and directness about the future of man. Christ only seldom prefaced His words with the expression, "Truly, truly, I say to you,"[2] and in this Gospel passage He repeats it twice, once at the beginning and once at the end of the discourse. This indicates the issue is extremely important—indeed, the ultimate purpose of the entire Gospel. The very center of the Lord Jesus Christ's teaching, the pulsating heart of His words, is contained in this discourse. Humanity has held tightly to this message from the moment it was uttered until this day. The Church was built upon it, and by it she is being renewed from generation to generation. And *you* are the fruit of this Gospel. The theme: the New Birth of Man.

---

1   John 3
2   In the NKJV this is translated, "Most assuredly, I say to you." The KJV is closer to the original with, "Verily, verily, I say to you." The Arabic translation is quite exact.

Is it even possible? After man has grown old in sin, and after his soul has become stifled by various transgressions intertwined and entangled together, can he still be renewed? It is really quite impossible, not only for man to eliminate sin or to alleviate its effects, but also to unravel them and cure the source of each particular one. Christ here enters the thick darkness that has encompassed man to preach a new and living way—that He grants man the opportunity to be born a second time. The absolute hope of mankind! This is the hope of every sinner burdened by a weary conscience, who, after a long moral slumber, suddenly awakens and finds himself drowning in a sea of error. Each one of you who has had this awakening in his past can understand the magnitude of grief and despair that confronts a soul that has realized the amount of sin it bears.

This is the thrust of today's Gospel. It's a Gospel of never-ending hope. It's a Gospel of the power given to man, the greatness of which all generations past have not been able to fully comprehend. This Gospel announces a new principle for man, which is capable not only of changing him from a sinful being to a righteous one, but also of allowing him to exchange a life in the flesh for a life in the Spirit.[3] He is transformed from a son of Adam to a son of God. How marvelous is this Gospel!

It is known, beloved, that during the first centuries of the Church, the person who desired to join the faith was put through a period of instruction that lasted the entire forty days of the Holy Fast. He received all the teachings that pertained to Christianity, with the exception of one department: the sacraments. It was prohibited for any Christian to discuss this issue with any person who had not yet entered the faith and received baptism. The sacraments of the Church were veiled from the candidates for baptism—who were called *catechumens*—and the candidates only heard of them under the name of

---

3   Rom. 8:5

the "mystical teaching" or "hidden teaching," because they were things that would be revealed to them in the process of time. In Latin this was called the *disciplina arcani*, which means the "secret discipline." This secrecy lasted till the sixth week,[4] and the beginning of this week was a time of great joy for the candidates, who came by the thousands; and that's why the Church made it a point to focus all its readings at that time on baptism. And the Gospel we read today was specifically for the catechumens; it was a salute and a welcome to them. They were now ready to learn about the sacraments, starting with baptism.

You may know that Nicodemus makes three appearances in the Gospel. The first time is in this passage, when he came to Christ at night using the utmost caution, to put forward questions plagued by doubts and reservations. The second time was during the meeting of the Sanhedrin, which hastily convened to sentence Christ to death.[5] Then he objected, saying the Law did not condemn a man before it had first heard his defense. They cast startled looks at him and said, "What's wrong with you? Are you also from Galilee? Did any prophet arise from there?" He became silent and withdrew from the scene— again, he was weak. The third time was when he accompanied Joseph of Arimathea during the burial.[6] He had finally plucked up courage at that time, while the disciples had fled into hiding.

We will be taking a good look at this personality today. Nicodemus is a symbol of the Old Man; he even says about himself, "How can a man be born when he is *old*? Can he enter a second time into his mother's womb and be born?"[7] Can the old man itself be born again? It's impossible, of course. Neither in Nicodemus's sense nor in the biblical sense of "old man" can the old man be born again. It can only *die*. The New Man must be born.

---

4   I.e., the week before Holy Week.
5   John 7:50–52
6   John 19:38, 39
7   John 3:4

The current generation is a reflection of Nicodemus. We are a doubting generation, full of hesitancy and reservation, that desires to live primarily by its intellect. I would like to ask this generation: What do you want to hear about today? Are you coming as Nicodemus, to increase your knowledge, or to hear some new thing?[8] This generation possesses a very big, conceited head, but its *heart* is weak. Even modern medicine says this is the generation of heart disease. You can have a man of sixty years who is a big-shot and the ruler of a country, who goes to the doctor and is told, "You have a fragile heart. It's afflicted by this-and-that." That's the case medically, but I say we have the same problem spiritually. Unfortunately, though, no one goes to the spiritual doctor saying, "My soul is sick." Beloved, this is the real diagnosis of this generation's spiritual state; we are a "Nicodemian" generation, one that only values bare knowledge.

"There was a man of the Pharisees named Nicodemus, a ruler of the Jews. This man came to Jesus by night and said to Him, '*Teacher*[9], we know that You are a *teacher* come from God; for no one can do these signs that You do unless God is with him.'"[10] All Nicodemus has in his mind is "teaching" and information. Is he coming to Christ as the Messiah? Or as the Son of God? Nothing of the kind. He's coming to Christ as a teacher like himself, as one of the same rank. Beloved, when we approach the Bible and attempt to analyze it merely on the intellectual plane, are we not doing as Nicodemus did? Let this not be, beloved! Today a new message is being given to you and to me; let us never again approach Christ by means of mere logic.

Nicodemus told him, "I'm a teacher like You, and I studied the Law like You, but I heard that You perform signs; that told me You must be a teacher come from God." It was known that any rabbi among the

---

8   Acts 17:21

9   The English translation has "Rabbi," but the Arabic has the equivalent "teacher."

10   John 3:1, 2

Jews must have received his teaching from a higher rabbi or from a school; and Judea at that time had a multitude of rabbinical schools. "You are a teacher come from God" meant that He had not formally learned in any of the rabbinical schools—a point that caught Nicodemus's attention—and yet he still approached Him as on the same level in order to acquire some knowledge. (Are *we* coming just to increase knowledge? It will never satisfy.)

Christ then responds by immediately cutting short his questionings and initiating a discourse. He says, "Unless one is born again, he cannot see the kingdom of God." It wasn't a direct response, and this is how Christ deals with us. He never, ever offers a *direct* answer. You may stand for over an hour talking to God from the depths of your heart, but the answer comes later in your day-to-day life. He doesn't respond to your words, but instead to your heart and intentions. Thus did Christ reveal the true intentions of the Pharisee who stood before Him.

Oh, that Christ would answer you and me like this today! When I was reading my Bible trying to figure out this Nicodemus, I grew ashamed of myself, because I realized I was acting just like him. I said, "Lord, forgive me, I do not desire to know anything. I want to speak about the Gospel and have *You* express the words and deliver the message. But to increase mere knowledge will profit us nothing."

Nicodemus approached Christ to increase his learning, but the Lord responded with vigorous words that had nothing to do with common "teaching" or knowledge or anything of the kind. He said, "No one can ever see the kingdom of God unless he is born from above." Beloved, the message to us this morning is the following: We all sit at the feet of the Church to learn from her, and we open our Bibles to increase knowledge; but beloved, this needs to be corrected and changed in us. "Truly, truly, I say to you": The Lord is speaking this to you. Do not seek to inflate your knowledge, for it will take you nowhere. The old cannot be placed on top of the new; the old must *die* in order for the new to be *born*. My child, you are called to live a totally new life!

✝ ✝ ✝

Notice that Christ offered His teaching to Nicodemus in degrees. He said, "Most assuredly, I say to you, unless one is born again, he cannot see the kingdom of God." Nicodemus said to Him, "How can a man be born when he is old? Can he enter a second time into his mother's womb and be born?" Take note of the word *enter*. Jesus continued, "Most assuredly, I say to you, unless one is born of water and the Spirit, he cannot enter the kingdom of God." In Christ's first statement, He said that unless one is born again, he cannot *see* the Kingdom. And in the second, when He wanted to emphasize the importance of water and Spirit, He said that without them one cannot *enter* the Kingdom. Let me pause here a moment to explain the difference between the *see* and the *enter*.

I will digress with you to the Old Testament and the story of Israel's exodus from Egypt. Israel's leader was Moses. He led them out of Egypt, which symbolized the province of darkness and Satan, to the Promised Land. Now a question: Did Moses enter the Promised Land? No. Another question: What was the extent of his relationship to the Promised Land? He *saw* it.[11] You see the mystical nature of John's Gospel! It requires its reader to have a very fine spiritual sense. Christ is trying to explain to Nicodemus that the Kingdom of God is like the Promised Land to those lost in the wilderness. The Kingdom of God is the life that is arranged and managed directly by God Himself; it is the homeland over which Christ reigns. So just as Moses

---

11 Deut. 34:4

wandered among the mountains intensely yearning to see the Promised Land—desiring for forty years just to glimpse it before he died—so does man yearn earnestly to see spiritual things.

The truth is that Moses was very dear to God, but he was a symbol of the Law. And can the Law gain us entrance to the Promised Land, that is, to the Kingdom? No; and since he symbolized the Law, God refused to allow him entrance. He said, "You will only see it from afar." The lawyers and Pharisees were the same; they saw it from afar, but would not enter.[12] But how could Nicodemus see it from afar? If he opened his heart to God, to understand the new teaching and accept the new birth, then he could at least die with the *hope* of the Kingdom. God raised Moses up on a high mountain so he could see the Land; and he saw it, and died on the hope.[13]

Unfortunately, Nicodemus still could not understand. Do you know why? Let me pause here and tell you his story. It's not written in the Gospel, but I will illustrate it for you to help you live the events with me.

The news began to spread one day that John the Baptist was baptizing; and the news reached the Pharisees, one of whom was Nicodemus. It was said, "John is baptizing, and the people are flocking to him. And when they are baptized, they repent and bear witness to God. What a great work is being done!" So the Pharisees murmured, "Oh no, certainly not, we could never run like little children to this Baptist. Who knows what school educated him? How can *we*—the lawyers, Pharisees, and rabbis, *we* the members of the Sanhedrin—go and bow our heads to *him*? Can *we*, the elders and wise men of Israel, lower our heads to *him*, a man of some thirty years, and be baptized? Never." Thus, "They rejected the will of God for themselves, not having been

12 Matt. 23:13; 5:20
13 Deut. 34:4

baptized by him."[14] Christ told them at another time, "John came to you in the way of righteousness, and you did not believe him."[15] Who then believed? The tax collectors and harlots! And so at another time He says to them, "I say to you that tax collectors and harlots will enter the kingdom of God before you."[16]

Notice that here He is speaking only regarding John's baptism. He said, "You, the Pharisees and leaders of Israel, have rejected the will of God for yourselves—have rejected John's baptism—while tax collectors, harlots, and sinners have believed and accepted John's baptism—they accepted God's will for themselves." Here Nicodemus disappoints us. He was one of those who rejected God's will for himself; and he who refuses God's will has his eyes blinded. As we said before, baptism is the opening of one's eyes. Nicodemus went to Christ *by night*—is this a hint from St. John that he couldn't see? Is this indeed a teacher of the Law coming by night? What a shame. Why could he not come by day? It was a sign of his doubting; *doubt* is a key factor in darkened eyes. But what was the origin of his doubt? The refusal of John's baptism.

Please pay close attention here, because this Gospel passage is very sublime. Christ told him, "Unless one is born again, he cannot *see*." He was saying, "You are coming to see more clearly, but you refused John's baptism. You can never see that way. I cannot help you, my friend. If an adulteress comes to Me, I can open her eyes and bring her into the Kingdom. If a sinning tax collector, like Matthew, comes to Me, I can bring him in. But as for you, the darkness has covered your eyes. How supremely unfortunate it is that you refused John's baptism."

This is why I am so deeply grieved, Abbas, that there are certain segments of Christianity that either don't believe in baptism

---

14   Luke 7:30
15   Matt. 21:32
16   Matt. 21:31

or don't recognize its significance in the way Christ required. They refuse God's will for themselves. "Why do we need water?" they ask. "The baptism by the Spirit is enough." But did Christ say that? Did Christ say that baptism by water is unimportant? Rather, when He spoke of the need to receive baptism from above, he equated it with the baptism of water and Spirit. He clearly placed the "baptism from above" and the "baptism of water and Spirit" on the same level. And the Church has joined the two baptisms into one—John's baptism of water and repentance for the forgiveness of sin, and the baptism by the Holy Spirit and fire.

Are these words touching our hearts? Are we approaching a new understanding of the second birth? We are all baptized, it is true. But something scares me. If I were able to remove these physical eyes of mine and put spiritual eyes in their place, and look into the face of each one of you, to penetrate his depths, would I find the perfect new man? Would I find the Word hidden within and producing fruit thirty-, sixty-, and a hundred-fold? Would I find the authentic new man, reaching unto the stature of the fullness of Christ; adorned with every grace; living and speaking in the Spirit; abiding in the humility and patience of Christ; bearing witness as a true son of God? Alas, as I gaze at some of you, I find the new man exceedingly small, with its mouth gagged and unable to speak. He makes not a sound nor a movement. Yes, Abbas, we have all been reborn; but there is one who has reached the stature of Christ in faith and wisdom and conduct, and another who is still very small and barely gasping for breath.

Again, are we really living as those born from above? Someone might respond, "Well, help us decide. Tell us what the man born from above does, and we'll see." I will tell you. St. Paul says, "If you are risen with Christ, seek those things that are above, where Christ is seated."[17]

---

17 Col. 3:1

In other words, it will be clear from what you *seek*. For example, a visiting youth might hand you a scrap of paper and say, "Quick, give this to Abba Matta before he enters his cell, so he can pray for me that I pass my examinations." Okay, my friend, may you pass. But "he who sows to his flesh will of the flesh reap corruption."[18] Christ Himself told us not to be anxious, neither concerning an exam, nor a lawsuit, nor anything else. "If you are My children, I will give you more than you need. Seek the Kingdom of God and His righteousness *first*, as those born for the Kingdom. Seek what endures forever, and leave the other little trifles to *Me*."

I will give you a spiritual law, beloved, and never forget it: Christ grants us the needs of the body even without a request; as for our spiritual needs, they can never be granted by God without a request. A person says, "Please, Abba, take these court papers and pray for us that God would rid us of this problem!" Yes, this type only cares about the world's concerns. But where is the concern for Christ, and where is the concern for the eternal homeland? Oh, believe me, beloved, it is by your *requests* that you will know if you are born from above or only born of the body. That which is born of the flesh is flesh, and that which is born of the Spirit is spirit.[19] You can distinguish which of the two dominates a person's life by the requests he makes.

Consider this verse: "As many as are led by the Spirit of God, these are sons of God."[20] It's a good verse, don't you think? What are you *led by*? Are you led by God's Spirit or by your fancies and desires? Only you can judge yourself on this point. I am able to judge you regarding the first point,[21] because your requests are obvious and they reveal your heart. But as for your *inner* leadings, only you can know what it

---

18   Gal. 6:8

19   John 3:6

20   Rom. 8:14

21   I.e., "It is by your *requests* that you will know if you are born from above or only born of the body."

is that directs you. Is it your knowledge? Your ego? Your lusts? Your money? Your anxieties? Or the Spirit of God?

Let me illustrate further. The person led by the Spirit will be sitting among you at a given time and will suddenly say, "Excuse me, Abba." You will ask, "Where are you going?" And he will respond, "I just have to take care of something and I'll be right back." He then enters his room and begins to pray. What has happened here? While he was sitting there, the Spirit breathed into him, and he felt an urgent need to hurry to his room and pray. This is a person who responds to the leading of the Holy Spirit.

Or again, there can be a person who, as a fast approaches, begins making excuses: "I'm feeling tired and ill lately, I can't fast this time." But once the fast has begun, you find him fasting. He tells you, "I couldn't take it; the Spirit was rebuking me! Though I feared growing weak and tired, now I feel none of these things." This type is led by the Spirit of God.

If the Spirit of God pleads with us to pray, let us pray. If He pleads with us to fast, let us fast. If it's to befriend someone, let us befriend him. If it's to read the Bible, let us read. From this kind of inward leading it is made clear whether or not you are led by the Spirit. Every person does the works of his father; that is, every person imitates the work of the one from whom he is born. Did you know that your father is the Holy Spirit? A person naturally carries out the wishes and directions of his father.

On the other hand, your father could be the flesh, with the ego that lays waste to your life, forcing you to exhaust yourself in becoming puffed up—in amassing knowledge, honor, money, etc. If those who are led by God's Spirit are children of God, then those who are led by pride and self-conceit follow someone else—but I don't want to mention his name, especially not today. When Christ sent out St. Paul on his mission, He told him, "Go to the Gentiles, and preach to them to turn them from darkness to light and from the power of Satan to God."[22]   When will we turn to You, O God? When will we turn from the power of Satan, and lust, and arrogance, and being puffed up? Whom do we worship? Whom do we follow after? "As many as are led by the Spirit of God, these are sons of God."

☩ ☩ ☩

"Abba, can you give a word to comfort us now?" Yes: "The Spirit Himself bears witness with our spirit that we are children of God."[23] What a splendid verse—the Spirit bears witness within us! "But what if He doesn't bear witness in me?" Ah, be careful! Be very careful never to let your relationship with God's Spirit drift in that direction! "Then tell me how He bears witness." I will.

Do you remember ever performing a "redemptive" act? An act of great self-sacrifice? Women are experienced in this. When a boy is sick, his mother is on her feet for two or three days straight tending to him. If he's in bed for a whole week, she's there for him; and if he needs so much as a tiny morsel of bread, she runs to fetch it. If you tell her, "Rest a little," she will say, "Rest? How can I?" This is sacrifice. But what motivates her? What drives and comforts her in her tireless activity? The Spirit bears witness within her that what she is doing is an act of God! A sense of God's work allows her to toil on her two feet without complaining. Or take a servant who walks all around town on his two feet ministering. One house rejects him, another kicks him out, another mistreats him, and he's all the while joyful! He receives honor from no one, but he never slacks in his service. The Spirit bears witness within him.

---

22 Acts 26:18
23 Rom. 8:16

Does the Spirit bear witness in us that we are children of God? Beloved, never forget that we are born from above. The word *above* is important, and I want to shed some light on its significance. Remember the verse, "You are from beneath; I am from above."[24] In Greek, "from above" is *ekto ano*, and "from beneath" is *ekto kato*. Those of you who understand electrical conduction know that current flows from the cathode to the anode. The anode is the positive charge, and the cathode is the negative. What happens when the anode and cathode interact? The light turns on.

We have spiritual *energy* in us. We have wonderful earthly virtues—scholarship, bravery, eloquence, human patience—these are cathodic virtues, that is, earthly and natural virtues. But imagine when these are touched by the positive charge: The light shines, the virtues are all illuminated and cause rejoicing, for "You are the light of the world."[25] You, in the physical body, you, with your natural abilities, once you are touched by the Spirit, you shine. This is the gift of the new birth. It makes the lifeless abilities and unlighted qualities to shine. They no longer serve Satan's purposes, but they serve Him who died and rose again.

What grace! Joy! Eternal happiness! Do you see that we've been made like Christ? We are no longer like the scribes and Pharisees who caused Him such grief. We are not of this world; believe me, we are not. And I will give you a verse for you to believe me even more. In John 17, Christ speaks to the Father about the disciples, saying, "They are not of the world, just as I am not of the world."[26] Ah, Christ's own testimony that they were born from above!

I fear, my beloved, lest we be given such treasures and still perform the deeds of the world. St. Paul says, "Therefore put to death your

---

24 John 8:23
25 Matt. 5:14
26 John 17:16

members which are on the earth,"[27] then goes into a depressing and revolting list of sins, including fornication, uncleanness, coveteousness, and so on. But I mourn deeply, and my voice cracks, because some of us do these things. These things are found in us! But how, O Lord, can this be? Can the light mingle with darkness? Can the new birth overlap with the old? Can I use a piece of cloth from a new garment to patch a tear in an old, tattered garment?[28] But it will take on the worn-out qualities of the old garment, and both will be made worse. Beloved, can the corruptible put on the incorruptible?[29] Can a spring of fresh water issue forth bitter?[30] Can a thorn bush produce grapes instead of thistles?

Beloved, I earnestly plead with you that we not perform the works of darkness and the deeds of the world! Let us never again grant authority to the old flesh. He says, "Put off the old man with his deeds,"[31] and "Be renewed in the spirit of your mind"[32] —by the living word, which is able to penetrate deep within and *change* us. We have all been reborn, but now we are in need of rediscovering our new birth. We need God's Word, beloved!

"But Abba," you might tell me, "I'm not an educated man. I'm old, and my brain is worn out. You monks are younger and have plenty of time to read." My friend, consider, if a family brings home ten to fifteen kilos of food one day, how many mere grams will their small boy eat? All he needs is three or four grams with a bit of water, and he's satisfied. So what is required of you is the reading of just three or four lines in the Bible, with full attention, in order to "nurse" your soul.

---

27 Col. 3:5
28 Mark 2:21
29 1 Cor. 15:53
30 Jas. 3:11
31 Col. 3:9
32 Eph. 4:23

Your young soul needs spiritual milk that it might grow up and know right from wrong. The tragedy is that we still don't know right from wrong! A person comes and says, "Abba, I don't want to pay taxes to the government. They're all a bunch of crooks who want to take our money." Ah, me! The new man is not awake and is not working. All this person sees is his heap of money and it being wasted on the government. You are sucking the blood out of the new man and causing him to die! My friend, give to Caesar what is Caesar's and to God what is God's. Allow him who is born of God to grow and increase. Let him increase and grow stronger, in stature, in faith, and in spirit!

I beseech Christ, who stands among us today as the Teacher, who admonishes the Nicodemus within each of us, that He might give life to the new man—whom He bore by His sufferings, His Cross, and His Resurrection—and that He might fill up the grace we received in the Mystery of Baptism, that we might live out our baptism, as well as our new life, every single day. I beseech Him that we might know precisely how to conduct ourselves, no longer as ignorant but as wise, redeeming the time,[33] transforming time into eternity. No other creature in the universe except man has been given the authority to transform time into eternity. The hour in which you stand to pray is itself transformed into eternal life. No other creature in the universe has been given the grace to transform dirt into the material of heaven. We change this dirt into flour and into holy bread, then offer it and eat it. Then with our knees, which were nourished by this dirt, we kneel and pray, thus pressing our natural faculties into the service, not of earth, but of heaven. What is this amazing power! What amazing grace!

Grant us, O Lord, to have the Holy Spirit within us, who changes what's corrupt in us to incorruption and who changes our fleshly desires to Kingdom desires. We ask the Lord, who gave us this

---

33 Eph. 5:16, 17

grace, to renew His work in us, that we might perceive the Kingdom for which we were born, and the eternal homeland to which we were called.

Walk in the Light

1977

Then Jesus said to them, "A little while longer the light is with you. Walk while you have the light, lest darkness overtake you; he who walks in darkness does not know where he is going. While you have the light, believe in the light, that you may become sons of light." These things Jesus spoke, and departed, and was hidden from them. (John 12:35, 36)

I have taken this verse out of the chapter's context, but it touches on many other verses and events in the same Gospel. St. John's Gospel strives to present Christ to us as the Light: "I am the light of the world."[1] In the first chapter, the Apostle speaks of Christ not as the common, everyday "light" we are used to, but as "the light that enlightens every man who comes into the world."[2] He *enlightens* man, not just gives light *to* man. If we contemplate Christ as our light, with the same simplicity that generally characterizes His relationship to us, we will find the concept easy.

---

1   John 8:12
2   John 1:9

When we opened the window, the room was filled with light. Once the light appeared, the darkness vanished. The mistake we tend to make is to think of these things only in philosophical, intellectual terms. If we wish to enter deeper into the understanding, or the real action, of what binds us to God, we must think in simple terms. By the illustration of the entrance of light into the room and the displacement of darkness, we begin to develop a practical understanding of the relationship that binds us to God.

Darkness was here; and when light entered, darkness was no longer here. But how? From where did it exit? It did not "leave" at all—it was the light that entered. Darkness does not "move." It has no real being, and is not capable of action. The entrance of light revealed the nothingness of darkness. The entrance of one ray of light defeats and "finishes off" the darkness. So it's very clear that darkness in and of itself has no being. It did not shift or exit in any way because of the light's entrance but rather was immediately displaced by the light. Light is motion, but darkness is non-motion.

My purpose here is to make us feel our relationship to Christ, to know the basis of our lives as Christians. The verse says, "Walk while you have the light." If the light is here, then let's begin walking. But if there's no light, "He who walks in darkness does not know where he is going." You see here that knowing is linked to walking. In darkness, both knowledge and walking are obstructed. So in Christ's absence, we don't know where to walk; our goal is completely unclear. But in His presence—"walk while you have the light."

Again, light is movement and progress. Where there is light, there instantly is motion. This contradicts the teaching that says meditation is sufficient for transporting us to God. Not at all. True contemplation—that which engages the mind, the heart, the entire being—instantly leads to a path to be walked. It's impossible to receive the light and remain stationary. The light will show me the way, and the way will require me to walk. Once I've received Christ, my path is immediately made clear. I must go forward, and I must say to the person who is just standing, "The light has come! Come along and I will show you."

It's like a blind man and a seeing man being in a dark room together. Once light enters, the seeing man sees everything around him, including the path. He takes the hand of the blind man and says, "Let's go." If the seeing man walks out alone, he will be judged. He will be asked, "After you saw the light, why didn't you take your blind brother's hand and lead him out?" So then, contemplation is indeed a basking in God's light, but it also immediately leads to movement.

When Adam was in the Garden of Eden, he was constantly contemplating God; he lived and moved in the truth. He was constantly growing and would eventually have grown into the fullness of the image in which he was created; but when his eyes shifted away from God and focused on his flesh and on matter, he immediately lost the vision of God. Once he saw the fruit, and how it was good for food and desirable to the eyes, he began to contemplate created things. His human eyes then took control rather than his vision of God. The contemplation of created things immediately bent his eyes toward his body, and he saw that he was naked. This is the most idealistic way to understand the Fall. Salvation, we may then say, is the contemplation of God, and sin and perdition are the contemplation of flesh and matter.

Therefore, if we lift up our minds and hearts—or the "eyes of our hearts," as the ancients used to put it—to the vision of God, that is salvation. It is salvation because it generates the walking in the way. Once you stand for prayer and lift up your heart to God, and your vision of Him opens up, you straightway receive spiritual fire and new blessings; and you will go out in sudden power, "having your feet shod with the Gospel."[3] You can never stand before God with a genuine

---

3   Eph. 6:15

and powerful vision of Him and not be moved. You will be moved in your soul; you will immediately ascend. For example, you will say, "Lord, I make with You this covenant, that I will never do this or that again," or, "Lord, I will never think in this or that way again." The contemplation of God immediately results in a movement from darkness into the light. So then, every contemplation of God leads to salvation, or rather, is itself salvation.

If man ceases his contemplation of God, or ceases prayer, or ceases lifting up his heart and conscience to God, he will find himself quickly contemplating the things of the flesh. As a result, the contemplation of God becomes difficult or unpleasant. Man feels that he is "fallen." And when you feel this way, you might say, "I'm living in sin. I'm far away from God. I'm fallen." The person who hears you might assume you've done something terrible; but that's not the case. When a person feels he is fallen, it's a fall from the height of the contemplation of God.

The contemplation of God involves two different aspects. The first is an unceasing inward movement—which we have termed "salvation"—from darkness to light, from the material to the divine. It's an inward movement, an existential[4] movement, whose direction is upward, and which lifts me above the world and above mind. But, as I said before, it is also a simple activity and does not require one to strain his mind. It is like telling a child outside a room, "Come in." The child does not complicate matters by asking how, and saying he isn't worthy, and so on. Rather, with perfect simplicity, we may enter God's presence like a child—with our dirt and defects and all that we are. We then find redemption, as well as an incredible inner transformation.

The second aspect is the fact that, once we are enlightened, we ourselves begin to illuminate. If I am sitting in darkness and then

---

4   In the sense that the "movement" involves a person's entire existence or being.

open my eyes, light enters my eyes, and my eyes themselves take on the nature of light. If my eyes can see the light, that means the light and the eyes have been united, and thence my eyes are enabled to see everything else. That is why when the new man (who is born of God) contemplates God, he enters the light and becomes one with it; and from that point he looks upon all things with a clear and bright vision—the direct opposite of the darkness that formerly made him stumble.

Since the entrance of light changes me to light, the result is that I begin to evangelize and save others; I begin to take others' hands and lead them into the light I've experienced. They begin to say, "My, how his face shines! His life has changed, and how it illuminates!" These are actually descriptions of the person who lives with God. Try going into your private room and praying for six or seven hours; when you come out, the grace will be evident in your eyes, your features, your actions—all without a word. Your silence itself will speak.

How does this happen? By my union with the light. I myself am nothing; I am naturally dark, but my union with the light makes me bright. Again, this happens with the simplicity with which a child walks into God's presence. It requires not intellect, nor method, nor logic, nor shrewdness, nor worrying about whether I'm worthy or not, whether I'm destined or not, whether I'm bad or good—all these things should not hinder our approach to God. Imagine a person sitting in a dark room being invited out into the light. Will he say, "No, I'm not worthy of the light"? No one ever says that, because the truth is, we're created for the light. If the person tells you, "Don't take me out. I prefer to sit in the dark," you will get him a psychiatrist, because he's not behaving as a normal human being.

We are created to be children of the light! Baptism is called illumination, because we are changed from children of darkness to children of the light. "In Him was life, and the life was the light of men."[5] We often stand to pray but are not filled with light. My message to you this morning is that every time you enter your room to pray, and every approach you make to God, is a call to receive the light—like the eye that is opened to allow light's entrance. Prayer is the reception of God Himself. We will never be able to understand God in the simple way the Bible presents Him to us unless we believe that God is light, and Christ is the ray of that light. The Bible describes God as "unapproachable light,"[6] and that is why Christ came as the ray and image of that light, which enters deep inside us.

When the church fathers used the sun as an expression of the Trinity, it wasn't a merely theological idea. It's an expression of the idea of our salvation. The eye cannot reach the Father, so Christ was incarnate and thus became a ray emanating from the light source—the Father—which we not only see, but it penetrates us to our inward depths. He has penetrated us by uniting with humanity; and so, after the Incarnation, the source of the "unapproachable light" has now become approachable. Even more, the Incarnation made the inaccessible being into a being we can unite with.

Look at John 17: "I in them, and You in Me."[7] This union we have with God is not a numerical union, nor a union of nature, but rather a union of vision, of presence, and of salvation. "It was impossible that they could ever approach You, O Father, unless I had taken on their flesh and dwelt in them, so that the light could enter them. I am in them, so the path to You is now laid open."[8] This is why He said, "I am the way."[9] The hidden depths of God have been revealed to us! And not only to us, but in us.

---

5   John 1:4
6   1 Tim. 6:16
7   John 17:23
8   Abba Matta paraphrases and expands on our Lord's words.
9   John 14:6

We have received God through Christ Jesus, but again, this union is not one of divine nature but simply of life. As we said, God is simple, and there is no division within Himself. Every division means duality, and duality means multiplicity; but in God there is no multiplicity. God is Father, Son, and Holy Spirit in a simplicity, not a multiplicity. That's why when Christ says, "The Father is in Me and I in Him, and we are One,"[10] He precludes any conflict or dualism; they are therefore one. We receive this simplicity within ourselves as light; and light knows neither division nor dualism.

So when we receive Christ, we enter into this simple oneness, and therefore there is found no division between us and God. Our will and God's will are no longer divided. "Thy will be done." We are one with the Father in Christ Jesus. This is something you cannot understand unless you "convert and become like little children"[11]—you can neither know God nor enter the Kingdom. We will also be able to understand this as long as we're not prohibited by a conscience weighed down by sin or burdened with guilt—all those things that prevent our interaction with the light and our vision of God. Even if God wishes to reveal Himself to us, He cannot when sin blinds man's eyes.

The great purpose of the Incarnation was to remove the barrier (sin) that blocks our entrance into the light. The removal of sin was accomplished in several different ways throughout our Lord's life: by teaching; by the repudiation of Satan and exposure of his works; and by the healing of man's eyes. When He opened the eyes of the man born blind,[12] this was a signal that He had come to heal man's spiritual eyes. The healing of the eyes of the blind has a critical connection to the opening of man's eyes to the vision of God.

---

10   See John 17: 22, 23.
11   Matt. 18:3
12   John 9

When the Pharisees were offended at His statement about the forgiveness of sins,[13] He asked them, "What is more difficult: forgiving sins, or telling this man to get up and walk?" Telling him to walk was really an easy thing; but to forgive his sins was an extremely difficult task. They couldn't understand the great and terrible price that was paid by the Father, before the foundation of the world, for the removal of that sin. When sin was removed from the crippled man's life, he rose. On the Cross, therefore, sin was conquered by Christ so that man could face the light.

Sin has not left the world. The "man of sin" is still present in this world, and the Prince of this World continues to beget sin in human nature. Despite all this, however, Christ removed sin as a final barrier between man and God. What this means is that the sinner can lift his eyes toward God and see Him. This barrier is the "blindness" we spoke of earlier, the absence of the knowledge of the Father. If we know the Trinity, it means we've been saved from sin. When you close your door with the intention of concealing yourself for prayer, it is only made possible by the removal of sin. Nothing can separate us from God! We are formally invited by Him to enter, at all times, into the Father's presence for prayer. We go in and out, in and out, with the same confidence a child has in entering his parents' bedroom without knocking on the door. If the mother says, "Yell at your son for coming in without knocking," the father will answer, "No, no, I can't do that to him. He's my son, not a servant. Let him come in and out as much as he wants!" Christ says, "I am the door";[14] and so we enter the Father's presence through Him.

If the mother says to her boy, "Come here, son, to speak with your father," and he runs to hide under the couch, she may respond, "Why are you so afraid of your father? You must have done something

---

13 Mark 2:5–7
14 John 10:9

terrible! Tell me what you've done." His heart beats as quickly as a bird's, and he runs off. She goes and finds that he's covered his father's desk with pencil marks. She didn't see him commit the offense, but just by his flight she knew he must have done something wrong. He committed a wrong that caused him to escape his sonship. He now feels himself to be an adversary to his father and thinks a hard spanking is undoubtedly on the way. The father then appears, and the son's heart is pounding as he cowers into a corner. The father says, "The desk? Is that all? Don't worry, my son, I can fix it or get another one! Come, come, it's all right." He then feels that his sonship did not change in the least. Of course, when he grows older, he laughs as he looks back, because he once thought his father would kick him out of the house and make him wander the streets just for defacing the desk.

It is the same with sin. Man may imagine he can void the sonship that ties him to Christ and the Father, but God tells him, "No, no, never. Come, come, my beloved. Why are you upset? You made an error? But don't you know that you're My son?" It is said, "All is yours, and you are Christ's, and Christ is God's."[15]

"I am the light of the world." When Christ came into the world, darkness was scattered, and God became known. He became known personally. It was not a mere intellectual knowing, nor a legal knowing (for the letter of the Law kills[16]), but a "connective"[17] knowing. This connective knowing is fellowship with light. When I open my eyes, the light enters me; I unite with the light, and by it I can see everything else. When Christ entered us, human nature entered Him, our nature was enlightened, and we were made worthy to receive the light without any hindrance. Man was once lost; he did not know the way to God. And even if the prophets declared the way, that knowledge

---

15 1 Cor. 3:23
16 2 Cor. 3:6
17 I.e., a knowledge that successfully connects us to God.

still did not connect man to God. But when Christ came, He came as the Way, as a ray of light shining down from the Father. He gave us the connective knowledge of the Father that scattered the darkness. The darkness was ignorance of the Father, an ignorance which essentially was an inability to reach Him and fellowship with Him.

The absence of the Father means the presence of Satan, though Satan has no positive existence. He is a negative label for darkness; and like darkness, he is immediately scattered by the light. Christ's Incarnation is an expression of the light radiating down from its source above. This was a dynamic action, much more dynamic than any action of man. He came, moreover, by announcement; the angel appeared and said that a Savior was born to the world and they would rejoice.[18]

Satan is merely the absence of Christ. His existence is fleeting. He has no real existence in himself. This is in sharp contrast to Manichean teaching, which says there are two equal gods, one of light and the other of darkness. Darkness has no god. It has a "prince" and leader, but it draws its existence merely from the absence of the true Presence, who is God. Satan is seen as a person who moves and acts and corrupts creation, but Christ's presence instantly produces Satan's absence.

This shows us the importance of a relationship with Christ; for if we were speaking of light and darkness in just a philosophical sense, it wouldn't matter much. But when I showed how Satan personifies darkness, and how sin is the absence of existence and righteousness, it is made clear how Christ overcomes sin. Sin represents a schism, a duality, within man; but this schism is healed by God. Therefore, so long as we live in God through prayer, so long as we enter the light, and so long as we partake of God's simplicity, the body will peacefully submit to the spirit, and a man will be reconciled within himself and will be reconciled to Christ.

---

18   Luke 2:11

The Tough Road of Spirituality

GREAT LENT, 1978

Therefore, since we have this ministry, as we have received mercy, we do not lose heart. But we have renounced the hidden things of shame, not walking in craftiness nor handling the word of God deceitfully, but by manifestation of the truth commending ourselves to every man's conscience in the sight of God. But even if our gospel is veiled, it is veiled to those who are perishing, whose minds the god of this age has blinded, who do not believe, lest the light of the gospel of the glory of Christ, who is the image of God, should shine on them. For we do not preach ourselves, but Christ Jesus the Lord, and ourselves your bondservants for Jesus' sake. For it is the God who commanded light to shine out of darkness, who has shone in our hearts to give the light of the knowledge of the glory of God in the face of Jesus Christ. But we have this treasure in earthen vessels, that the excellence of the power may be of God and not of us. We are hard-pressed on every side, yet not crushed; we are perplexed, but not in despair; persecuted, but not forsaken; struck down, but not destroyed—always carrying about in the body the dying of the Lord Jesus, that the life of Jesus also may be manifested in our body. For we who live are always delivered to death for Jesus' sake, that the life of Jesus also may be manifested in our mortal flesh. So then death is working in us, but life in you.

2 Corinthians 4:1–12 NKJV

I am convinced that God has provided us with these words to serve as a source of support for us during these holy forty days of fasting. When we fast, or pray, or struggle, this passage is a guide toward the fulfillment of the ministry God has given us. Now we cannot fully explain the meaning of God's Word without relating one passage to another. In the previous chapter, it speaks about the ministry of the Law and how it was hidden by a "veil." A veil not only hides the truth about something but also blinds the person who is looking.

St. Paul is thus describing two types of ministry. The first was the ministry of the "letter," promulgated by Moses, which Israel mechanically utilized with the assumption that it could bring salvation without the need for spiritual progress. The other was the ministry of "glory," promulgated by Christ. And St. Paul makes the point that, whereas Moses' face shone while practicing the ministry of the Law—a face bound to die and putrefy in the grave—Christ's ministry of glory causes our *hearts* to shine from within.

The old ministry was one of animal sacrifice and law; and it had its professors who specialized in the law, who regulated the rules and restrictions that surrounded the Sabbath, as well as the rest of the Old Testament's ceremonies. But *we* have been given a new type of ministry. It has no law; it's an *inward* ministry, touching the *heart.* Since we have been given this ministry, let us not fail in it; indeed, since we have the ministry of the Spirit, we *cannot* fail. If we still had the ministry of the Law, we would be one hundred percent certain that failure awaited us. So if you intend to serve Christ by the works of the old Law, or by the punctilious keeping of the letter, thinking *that* will bring you into the Kingdom, you are making a most serious error. Only the Holy Spirit, only mystical enlightenment, only a generous heart, and only the knowledge of Christ can take you there.

What will provide us with light, therefore, is not the external rites carried out by the body, but the internal heart. Not only will we not fail, but moreover we must *renounce* the false worship. Israel had its ceremonies, its councils, its priests going hither and thither, its daily worship, all giving the impression that the nation was functioning properly—but God's wrath was upon them. All their vaunted wealth and worship were rejected, because a veil separated them from God. There is this severe danger in the ministry of the letter, because a man may appear outwardly pious while being inwardly corrupt. But the new worship—that of Christ Jesus—is not based on performances and facades. God is the one who originally commanded the rites and delivered them to the prophets; but once men seized exclusively upon the outward forms and became inwardly deranged, all this was rejected by Him.

The law in itself was a high honor granted to man, but in Christ we have been given mercies far greater. This is why Paul—who was a Pharisee and the son of a Pharisee; a member of the Sanhedrin; after whom people ran chanting "my lord, my lord," and carried the fringes of his robes, as they do today for the metropolitans of large cities—about such things Paul says that though he once considered them gain, he afterwards saw them as utter loss, in comparison to gaining Christ. Why, what have you found in Christ, O Paul? You were a member of the Pharisees and the Sanhedrin, and an intimate friend of the high priest, to the extent that you could secure a signed letter from him, as well as a detachment of temple guards, to accompany you in your persecutions of the Christians. What power you had! What influence! What, then, did you find in Christ?

This is what I found: "We are hard-pressed . . . perplexed . . . per-secuted . . . struck down . . . always carrying about in the body the dying of the Lord Jesus!" So the ministry of the New Testament is not one of luxuries. This service in Christ Jesus, to which Paul was appointed by God and which he was destined to make clear to all fol-lowing generations, is really a very peculiar one. *We are hard-pressed on every side.*

You may come to me and say, "Abba, I am very distressed," to which I will respond, "And?"

"How can I be living in this monastery with you, Abba Matta, and be in this distressed state?"

"Well, if you are to live the true Christian life, you will encounter even greater distress."

"What? I came here to be happy. They told me that monastery life is full of pleasure and good times. Christian life should be pure rejoicing."

"Indeed, whoever told you that is a liar."

We are hard-pressed on every side—but since we minister in the Spirit, since we no longer live for the flesh as in the former days, and since our hope is heaven, we do not fret. We are not crushed. I'm embarrassed to use the following example, but when we decide to fast till six or nine o'clock in the evening, we have begun on the way of "distress," though it is only an infant's step. Again, I'm embarrassed to say that fasting, service, toil, struggles, and the like are all just the first taste of being *hard-pressed on every side.* But such is Christianity; and such is our spiritual ministry. Would you (like Paul) prefer to go down this path, or to be a Pharisee and prominent member of the Sanhedrin?

We are not only hard-pressed on every side, but also *perplexed.* It's a perplexity[1] that never ends! This is the state David found himself in when he cried out, "I said in my haste, 'All men *are* liars.'"[2] Hard questions perplex us. What is truth? Where is justice? When I show love, why am I shown hate in return? Indeed, welcome to Christianity. *Perplexity!* You see, the rules of this world are governed by human logic. One plus one makes two. Play the market right and you'll be a success. Study hard and you'll pass. But the rules of the spirit are not decided by human logic. One plus one can make just one again; and a thousand years are as brief as yesterday.[3] Everything is flipped upside-down in spiritual life. You must know well that the ministry of the Spirit is not subject to human logic. Don't ever try to interpret it so.

Once you say, "This isn't fair," you've stepped outside the realm of the spirit and stepped into the realm of the law. "But how about the rules of fair play?" You want rules of fair play? Then take off your monastic garb, put on regular clothes, and go live in the world. For he who has donned this garb no longer has "rules of fair play." You have only enemies. Can you go to Satan and say, "Please be honest"? No; you have to deal with treachery and deceit and back-stabbing and kicks to the stomach while you're on the ground. You have entered on what is called unseen warfare, and there are no rules that govern it. It's all about deception and subterfuge. Didn't Paul say, "Be sober and vigilant, because your adversary the devil walks about like a roaring lion, seeking whom he may devour"?[4] How wicked is this creature! I would sooner battle a hundred natural lions than battle this

---

1   The Arabic word for *perplexity* has an Eastern coloring that gives it a more profound and multidimensional depth than the mere idea of mental confusion that is conveyed by the English term. In the Arabic, the state of perplexity touches the heart and the very foundations of one's being, where the acute experience of such a state can dislocate a person's entire soul.

2   Ps. 116:11

3   Ps. 90:4

4   1 Pet. 5:8

one unseen lion. I can arm myself against a natural lion and shoot at him from a distance; but Satan approaches by stealth during my prayers and strikes me.

So spiritual life is not regulated by orderly and predictable laws. There is no *why* in spirituality. You have *duties,* but no *rights.* Welcome to the Christian life! Don't go searching for reasons and explanations. Don't judge things before the proper time. The proper time for judging all things is *after* this life is over. The secrets of men's hearts will be revealed, and the true intentions of each man's heart will be displayed by God.[5] But for now, you cannot absolutely distinguish what is evil from what is good.

"We are *perplexed.*" I love that phrase. We're perplexed by the outward appearance of things, by religious systems, by the visible Church on earth, even by Christ Himself. For where is Christ to be found on earth? Where is real Christianity? Satan appears victorious. The cross is lifted once again, and Christ is being crucified. The world has forsaken Him. Apostasy is everywhere. Entire nations have gone astray. *Perplexity!* But it's a perplexity similar to that which afflicted the prophet Elijah. He thought all faithful men had disappeared from the earth and that he was left alone. But God told him, "No, no, don't burden yourself with such thoughts; I have thousands of My own hidden away."[6]

In just this way, when it comes to spiritual life, the use of earthly logic or analysis plunges us into utter perplexity. Therefore, Paul says, we are perplexed, *but not in despair.* We see before us the perils, and sins, and waywardness, along with the bitter consequences they will bring upon the Church; and Satan waiting to swallow the believers—and though these things make us terribly perplexed, yet we are never in despair. We know that He who conquered death can also conquer

---

5   1 Cor. 4:5
6   1 Kin. 19:18

sin. Cannot He who raised Lazarus from the dead raise the world from its sin?

You have all heard this remark from me many times before, and I will say it again, though it's a type of boasting on my part; but it is a boasting of weakness, or of that which is lacking in me.[7] Nobody has suffered more from such perplexity than I have. Everything that takes place around me I deeply consider and contemplate, by the light of the Bible and by the light of God's dealings with man. I have read copiously about the hard issues of life and pondered them thoroughly, and I say, no one is more perplexed than I.

Nevertheless—I have said this often, too—I never despair. Why? Because I will never be able to adjudicate spiritual matters with my human reason. Once the mind has reached its furthest possible point in solving life's perplexities, I say to it, "Stop right there. That's enough for you. Go to sleep now and wait for the morning to rise peacefully." Then I lay my head down until the glow of morning sunshine, and a new day brings to me a radiant joy.

The mind cannot but be perplexed, because everything is backwards; because the truth is evident and men trample it under their feet; because love, the extremely precious gift, is absent. Do you want to know how precious love is? Imagine Christ sitting here among us. We would be required to approach Him and kiss the holy body, as well as to kiss each other with joy. But He is present among all the churches, and they step on Him, each claiming to be superior to the rest. They envy each other, disparage each other, and accuse each other of error. What a perplexing chaos! However, we cannot give the mind the final word; we shall never grant human logic the right of pronouncing the final judgment on the case.

✛ ✛ ✛

---

7   2 Cor. 11:30

"We are persecuted, but not forsaken." It is a fact that, when a farmer raises a brood of small white chicks, if he introduces a reddish chick into the brood, they will assault the stranger and peck it to death. In other words, they will *persecute* the reddish chick. But why, we may ask? Isn't it a chicken just like the rest? Don't they share the same nature? But there's no compromise possible; they *must* persecute it. It is an eternal law: The sons of the flesh will persecute the sons of the spirit. Those who live after the manner of the flesh and its desires, after the manner and principles of this world, can scarcely tolerate those who live according to the spirit. In fact, they cannot stand them. This is why there has never been a spiritual person who could live at ease. Look at the martyrs, at the suffering saints, and at the tears and pains of all those who have gone upon the narrow way. Why were they persecuted? Because they looked different in this world.

Would you like to avoid persecution? Then take on the appearance of this world. "No man could buy or sell except he that had the mark or the name of the beast."[8] Place the mark of the prince of this world upon your arm, and you will buy and sell prosperously, and gain for yourself accolades and fame, and be promoted by the world. On the other hand, if you live faithfully by the Spirit, you will take on a new appearance and meet with certain persecution. It is a spiritual law: "The son of the bondwoman shall not be heir with the son of the freewoman."[9]

Watch what happens, for example, if there appears a monk in the monastery whose every other word is "Jesus," whose heart is full of Jesus, and who talks of nothing else but Jesus. You'll find the other monks beginning to mock him. I'm not even saying the people of this world will mock him, but rather the people of the monastery. When just one person begins to lead a really saintly life, and the signs of

---

8   Rev. 13:17
9   Gal. 4:30

heavenly grace begin to show on him, and the gifts and talents of the Holy Spirit start working through him, you'll find the other monks beginning to oppose him. That's how it is—the more a person develops a warm faith in Christ, the more the world resists him. His very siblings will provoke him.

How many times have I heard in confession the complaints of someone whose mother was antagonizing him only because he wished to serve his Church! "My family has been pushing me to indulge in the entertainments of this world, but I resisted; so my parents have insulted me, my sister has spat in my face, and they have treated me like scum." Christ's words are true: Once a person begins to receive the new life, his own family will persecute him.[10] Can you believe that a mother would ridicule her own son and spit in his face, abuse him with language so obscene that I cannot even repeat it, and take her other children to enjoy the amusements of this world while he sits in his room, alone and discouraged? And then they return home and bang on his door and raise a tumult of noise in order to disrupt his prayers.

So he came to me and said, "I just don't know what to do. I'm losing my mind." I told him, "But that's exactly what the Bible taught would be the case." He looked incredulous and asked, "Is it really? I thought I was the crazy one." I replied, "Not at all. You have just begun the Christian life."

And as I said before, the same happens here in the monastery as well. If a monk rises just a little bit above the rest in spiritual life, the others will give him a hard time. Are you prepared for that? We are about to start the Great Fast; we are entering the season of asceticism and worship; we will look at the glory of the Lord with unveiled faces;[11] we will be offering our fasting, our prayers, our tears, and our

---

10 Matt. 10:34–36
11 2 Cor. 3:18

entire selves as a sacrifice to God. We will unquestionably be changed. So the consequences await us. But as it is written, we are persecuted but not forsaken. It is impossible for a man who is being persecuted for Christ's sake to become weak. You will find him stronger than all. His persecutors become irritated at his inherent toughness, because he cannot be broken. He, however, feels himself to be meek and prays, "Lord, help your poor servant, for I am smaller than them all! They will destroy me!" You will be amazed at how much God's aiding strength will rain down on such a man. It strikes fear in the hearts of his adversaries.

"We are struck down, but not destroyed." This is the next logical step the adversary takes after he has begun the persecution—to strike at the believer and throw him to the ground. He will strike at his body, his soul, his dignity, his reputation, his character, or anything else in order to cast him down. When this happens to you, you lie prostrate on the ground before the gaze of everyone around, appearing like a vile person who deserves his lot. The people who threw you down assume that you're destroyed and done for; but then, surprisingly, they find you tenfold stronger and more alive than you were beforehand. And you yourself feel tenfold more robust than you were previously. I tell you it is impossible for this world's persecution to destroy the children of God! There is no form of persecution this world can invent—even if it arises from its greatest kings and armies—that is capable of destroying even a single weak believer. Utterly impossible. This is a divine promise to those who have accepted the ministry of the Spirit: *We are struck down, but not destroyed.*

"Always carrying about in the body the dying of the Lord Jesus." This is the finale and completion of all the foregoing persecutions and hardships. The marks of death begin to become visible in the body. That is, from the constant force of adversity applied by this world, the physical body begins to buckle under the pressure. The wounds of Christ's death appear—exhaustion, perplexity, pain—but we carry about this dying of the Lord Jesus *that the life of Jesus also may be manifested in our body*. Each pain that afflicts us speaks of the power and Resurrection of Christ Jesus living within us! All who have lived in Christ, and suffered in Christ, and carried the dying of Christ, become witnesses to Christ and bearers of His Resurrection.

How beautiful are the martyrs, whose very wounds converse about Christ! How wonderful are the suffering saints—who went about hungry, naked, lonely, and strangers on the earth—who were moved by love for Christ! In the end, the "dying" of these saints becomes something sweet and worthy of being kissed. The very ashes of these saints are worthy of reverence. Their agonies are a picture of glory. "Carrying about in the body the dying of the Lord Jesus, that the life of Jesus"—*His very life*—"also may be manifested in our body." Christ's martyrs are witnesses not just to His agonies but moreover to His *life*. This means that if there is a man who bears the dying of Christ, his life's story can never die and become extinct: rather, it will break out and expand, and produce new saints. His life's walk will resuscitate others' souls, will awaken others' consciences, and will renew the lives of other people who were on the road to death. These are the lives of the saints which I am always urging you to read.

"For we who live are always delivered to death for Jesus' sake." St. Paul presents this as a dogma of sorts. All that he explained beforehand was something of a *story*, describing the difficulties and pains he had encountered; but now he concludes with a *doctrine*, that is, a law with an authority over human life similar to that of any civil law. Consider a prosecuting lawyer who stands before a judge and says, "Based on law number such-and-such, the accused must be given such-and-such a sentence for his act." The law, in other words, tells the judge whether the criminal should live or die. But can the criminal code really have so much power? Yes; go observe the court system and see for yourself. Again, a defending lawyer tells a judge, "I request the application of law number such-and-such, which was cited in criminal trial number such-and-such, in such-and-such a city; and based on the foregoing facts, along with the witnesses and testimonies adduced, I plead innocence for my defendant." The judge finds that a watertight case has been made, from which he cannot budge an inch, and so hands down a verdict of innocence. "My goodness!" people respond. "What a high-powered attorney!" Not at all; it is not the attorney who is powerful, but the law itself. The law is what pronounced the defendant innocent.

Here, then, I am handing to you a veritable law, a dogma, a doctrine, all of which mean the same thing. For our doctrine is a collection of life-giving laws. If you live according to the doctrine, you will live; if you do not—well, let us not press that point right now. Our doctrine decrees that we be always delivered to death for Jesus' sake, that His life may be manifested in our bodies. But to do this, you must be perpetually conversant with the Bible.

Consider this verse: "Do not be conformed to this world, but be transformed by the renewing of your mind."[12] Tell me, how can you be transformed except by boldly confronting that ego of yours, which has proved such a vehement and inveterate adversary of your salvation? To help you do this, I put you to do work; and if grace helps us, I put you to particularly hard work. And you will come out with your ego vanquished. You will discover its faults, its stubbornness, its swollen pride, and its lies, until little by little it is dismantled. I must honestly say that, when I assign a monk to a particularly rough and distasteful task, my mind is burdened for his sake, and I follow his progress hour by hour. But in the end he comes out a real man.

St. Paul's words are clear: "*always*—at all times—carrying about in the body the dying of the Lord Jesus." So if there is ever to be found

---

12 Rom. 12:2

a time when you are not carrying His dying, consider it an empty and useless time in your life. Whether it be a day, a month, or a year, erase it completely from your life's history. For any period in your life in which you did not bear testimony to the Lord Jesus in your body, deem it a period missing from your spiritual life's past. For what else is Christianity? What else is this faith? Do not make the mistake of assuming it's all about contemplation and nice religion. It's rather about struggle, and toil, and mortification of the self.

I once sent out a monk to do the work of evangelism in a distant country, and he came back after a while and said, "I'm tired of this. I want to come back to the monastery and rest." I told him, "Of course you may." He replied, "Really? Thank you so much, Abba." I continued, "Yes, but you must know something. You will be emptied of all distinction." "What do you mean?" he asked. I said, "I mean you will be the most minor of the monks and will sit at the end of the table. You will once more be considered a pure novice." He replied, "Ah, no, Abba; then let me go back and resume my evangelism!" He reckoned his evangelism to be an earthly task when it was actually a spiritual task. But God raises for Himself manly sons by such work.

Tell me, do we wash the dishes here, or sweep the floor, or take out the garbage merely because the monastery needs it? No! You have a mission to fulfill far greater than the completion of these menial tasks. That other monk had returned to the monastery to feel the calm atmosphere, the nice green grass, and the steaming hot beans, and concluded that his work in the remote province was a mere wasteful toil compared with the life of repose he could enjoy here. Repose is easy. To lead a relaxed life of comfort is the easiest thing for me to allow for you. Much more difficult is it for me to turn you over to a lifestyle of effort and toilsome work. *That* costs me sweat and anxiety. It costs me sleepless nights, and concern over your lot and your advancement in the spiritual life!

So our calling in life is to "carry about in the body the dying of the Lord Jesus, that the life of Jesus also may be manifested in our body." This is the very meaning and substance of our lives as monks, or rather, as Christians. We are called to be *witnesses* to Christ. Monasticism itself is neither the beginning nor the end nor the zenith of the Christian life. The sum of monasticism is to be a witness to Christ. If you are not moving forward in your witness to Him, where are you going? That black garb you are wearing will not save you. Your beard will serve no purpose in heaven. Even your monastic name will not avail you above, for you will receive a *new* name.

Let us remember St. Paul's words as we now stand at the threshold of Great Lent, because, as you know, it is the springtime of the monk's life. I wish one day the spirituality of the Great Fast would grow and expand and fill up the greatest margins of our entire lives!

The Meaning of the Psalms

1973

As I promised you, we will begin to study the books that guide us along the way of salvation. And we will begin with the Psalms, because they serve as our daily food throughout life. As I have learned in studying it, the Psalter has been a source of consolation and blessing for the Church since the days of Moses until now. It has given strength, comfort, and support to the Church at all times. It is the Psalms that pulled the Church through prior ages.

The concept of "praise" had greater weight in Old Testament times than it does now. I am not referring to greater theological weight, but to our own deficiency in the use of the Psalter. In the Old Testament, the Psalms were offered as a living sacrifice or an audible sacrifice, the "praise of the lips," as St. Paul says.[1]

Sacrifice held a position of great significance in Old Testament worship, as it required extraordinary effort to carry out. Can you imagine the work involved in slaughtering and roasting one thousand

---

1   Heb. 13:15

lambs? And despite the complex intricacy of the sacrificial rituals, along with the amount of learning required of the priests, the "sacrifice of praise" occupied an equally important role in Old Testament worship.

I can't go into a full explanation of Old Testament praises now, because it would require us to review many little details and statistics to make an accurate picture; but there is one quick fact about the Psalms I want to discuss. The Psalms that were offered up to God in the Old Testament can be divided into two groups: those composed before the Captivity, called "pre-exilic," and those composed afterwards, "post-exilic." Each group possesses distinct characteristics, and you will rejoice when I give you the keys to understanding to which group any psalm belongs. You will encounter a serious error in some modern academic works which says the Psalter was composed only in the second-Temple era. This is a completely false notion, because the Psalms were used for praising during the first-Temple era as well. The first Temple is that which stood before the Captivity, and the second Temple was the renovated structure which stood after the Captivity.

The Psalms cover a time-span of about seven hundred years. The amazing thing is that, despite this long time period, the Psalms appear to the reader as if written by a single author. The popular idea is that David composed all the Psalms, but the truth is that many different authors contributed to their making; and even those attributed to him—"A Psalm of David"—were simply either collected by his hand, or sung by him, or arranged by him for liturgical worship. The 150 Psalms were collected by the Church in their present form approximately three hundred years B.C. (and by "Church" here I'm not distinguishing between the Old and New Testaments). Again, many scholars say the Psalms were still being composed well into the first century A.D., but this is a mistake. Around the year 300 B.C., the Psalms were translated in the Septuagint,[2] which we have in our hands with all 150 Psalms.

☩ ☩ ☩

Let's now talk about the meaning of the Psalms in our lives. We are monks, and a monk is someone who has voluntarily made himself a stranger on the earth. The Psalms console the stranger. For example, it's a beautiful experience to read the psalm written by the river of Babylon. It's quite obvious it was written during the Captivity: "By the rivers of Babylon, there we sat down, yea, we wept when we remembered Zion. We hung our harps upon the willows in the midst of it."[3] We do not have harps, but we make music with our tongues. And we do not have mirth, but instead sorrow; however, the Psalms transform the state of sorrow in our hearts into a state of prayer.

As I said, the Psalms are the monk's consolation. When the Holy Spirit prepared this book for the saints, it was designed to speak to every aspect of the human condition: joy and sorrow, hardship and plenty, strength and weakness, persecution and authority. Every circumstance man passes through is addressed in the Psalms. It is a book for all of life, a companion that comes alongside man every step of the way.

If a monk has placed it in his heart to be a citizen of heaven, then he will continually live for the sake of the Kingdom. In such a case, *time* is not seen or treated by him in the same way it is by a person in the world. For the world's citizen, each second has a monetary value, and time is something to be struggled with for the sake of earning one's bread and for the sake of earthly needs. But for heaven's citizen, time

2 The Greek version of the Old Testament, translated in Alexandria in the time of the Ptolemies, and famously said to have been rendered by seventy-two scholars sent by commission of the high priest in Jerusalem.

3 Ps. 137:1, 2

doesn't play such a role; it is meant to be transformed into something greater. An hour for him does not equal a given amount of money, or a given number of loaves. It's not something to be "transacted" in any worldly sense, but instead to be changed into something possessing heavenly value. These words might bear somewhat of a theoretical or philosophical tinge, but they pertain to our lives. St. Paul says, "Redeem the time, for the days are evil."[4] Everything I just said is an explanation of St. Paul's verse—which he wrote originally to people living in the world.

"Redeem the time." To *redeem* means to purchase it and transform it into something else, namely, into heavenly currency. This currency equals eternal life. I am to transform my temporal life into eternal life; I am to change these regular hours and nights and days into the content of eternity. How is this done? By prayer and the Psalms. When I pray a given hour of time, I am converting it into an hour of eternity. I say, for example, to a given hour of time, "Hello, what's your name?" It answers, "My name is the third hour of the day."[5] I ask, "What does that mean?" It answers, "This is the time the sun rises and people go to work to make money." I respond, "No, no: rather to me, you are the hour in which the Holy Spirit descended.[6] I must pray." I then exit worldly time, enter my cell, close the door, and become like the dead—just like the larvae that enters its silken cocoon and appears to have died. Similarly, the man who desires to offer up praise (the monk) enters his cell, then emerges donning new colors; he has transformed a trivial bit of time into an eternal weight of glory.

Imagine a diligent monk who completes the seven hours of prayer

---

4 Eph. 5:16
5 The third hour in Orthodox (or Jewish) prayer corresponds to our 9 A.M.
6 In Coptic liturgics, the third hour commemorates Pentecost (Acts 2:15).

of each day, that is, he covers all twenty-four hours.[7] He converts the whole day into eternal life, and he rejoices because he feels fulfilled and alive by virtue of completing what's important to him. As for the monk who doesn't complete his canonical hours, he reaches the end of the day in a state of hollow boredom and begins to question his purpose in life. He comes and asks me, "What is a monk's mission in life?" And I, in my simplicity, assume that this person is completing all his prayers, so I begin to expound the answer at length—whereas what he really needs is to return to the elementary principles of monasticism. He needs me to tell him, "Abba, don't ask me that question now. Go first to your cell and pray the seven hours correctly, then come back to me in two or three months and we'll talk." Then he goes and returns saying, "I have no more questions." He has realized that the monk is made for prayer, and by prayer he has understood his life's purpose.

This is why I am telling you with all earnestness that prayer, and especially prayer of the canonical hours, is of the utmost importance. Never believe any person, no matter how holy he may appear, who tells you it's okay to neglect your canonical prayers and Psalms because you must be "free" during prayer. Such is a false teacher who, having failed in his monasticism due to his negligence of his spiritual rule, desires to hide his laziness and drag others down with him. It is impossible for a person to neglect his prayers and still remain happy. You will find hints of anxiety lurking in his life. And no matter how much he tries to conceal them, they will rise to the surface every so often.

You might ask, "Is it really possible, Abba, for a person to do nothing else but to offer up praise?" I answer that, if you can achieve that state, then you will have arrived at the pinnacle of your life. Moreover,

---

7   In the Coptic canon, the twenty-four hours of each day are divided or distributed over seven "hours" of prayer.

you *must* reach that state. You might have obligations in life that compete with your prayers, but they are merely peripheral. If a monk is a doorkeeper, for example, the advice to him is to sing praises as he stands by the door. He tries it, finds it a delightful thing, and enters into a flight of happiness. Therefore, if we are able to successfully conquer time—if such a word can be used—to swallow it whole and completely submerge it in the liturgy, we will truly become like angels on earth. And at that point, our lives will be filled with comfort and joy without measure. Think of the hour or two you stand on your feet during the midnight praises: If you receive so much pleasure from that bit of toil, imagine the sheer magnitude of joy you would know if such worship and praise involved no toil at all and were easily sent up at all hours of the day! The only thing left for the monk at that point would be to sprout wings and fly.

As I said, do not heed any voice that tells you to forget about the Psalms or about any prayer that is merely "routine." This is a new word I've been hearing from this generation, a poisonous word, one I consider to be coming straight from the devil. Satan has been muttering it in people's ears, and they come and ask, "What's the point of *routine*, Abba? Anything routine is boring." Routine is, in fact, the very channel through which heavenly blessings will come to you. As the saints have said, without consistent prayer, it is impossible to receive the gifts of grace. As much as a person turns his heart and mind toward Christ in prayer, so much does he change into His image, even if he doesn't perceive it. This is especially true if there is no burden on the heart to act as a barrier to prayer—such as the anxieties or desires of the world—and if the heart is simple, and immersed in the Spirit, the person will definitely be changed by prayer.

✝ ✝ ✝

God reveals Himself to man in stages. God's revelation of Himself, for example, in the days of Abraham differed from that in the days of Moses, which differed from that in the time of David, which differed from that in the time of Malachi. When God reveals Himself, it is through the Spirit, who descends upon man, and the Spirit's action is in proportionate measure to a man's spiritual state.

Now the Psalms, which were composed over the course of seven hundred years, vary in the range of their depth and message. So just as God used the natural passing of large epochs of time to progressively reveal Himself to mankind, so does every person evolve in his relationship with God. The start you make with God is not the same as the end of your life with Him. Every day the relationship is renewed, and deepened, and changed. In the Psalms we find such stages that correspond to man's spiritual growth.

You might ask, "So if I'm praying the same psalm every single day, am I not making progress?" But we must beware of such unnecessary questions that lead to unprofitable answers. As you pass through the Psalms, you might come to one that does not "open up" to you; and then you arrive at a different psalm that does open up to you and moves you deeply. You stand before it for a while, amazed at how clearly you can discern its depths. What has happened? These experiences don't happen by chance. When you passed by the first psalm, your spiritual state—at that particular day and time—was not in accord with it. But your spiritual state *was* in accord with the second psalm. It did not open up merely because you spent more time with it and insisted on learning from it.

This is an important point: The second psalm benefitted you because you were standing in the spirit to pray with a full readiness to be moved any way the Spirit led. So you pass by one psalm, then another, until you arrive at a particular one that arouses your soul, and an inner stirring occurs, mingled with great joy. At that moment, your spiritual state was in accordance with that psalm. You will gain very much in those moments, and the gaining leads also to a changing.

But the next day you might return to that psalm and find nothing to gain, and you will tell yourself, "Dear me, my spiritual state today must be dreadful." No, it's not necessarily your defective spiritual state; it's just that the psalm has again become unproductive for you that day; however, there is another psalm awaiting you that will benefit you.

Now, what if you stand to pray, and *none* of the psalms opens up to you? In that case you are in need of self-examination; you are not living in the Spirit. Consider it like the thermometer the doctor puts in your mouth. If the temperature is elevated, he knows a foreign body has entered the patient's body and is causing a disturbance. Exactly so, when we come to pray and feel moved on the inside, then we are standing in the Spirit, and we are sure to receive our proper nourishment from the prayer.

✛ ✛ ✛

We must also understand that the central figure around which every psalm revolves is the Person of Christ. In the Old Testament we call Him "Messiah," and in the New Testament we call Him "Christ." The essential core of the Psalms, I say, is Messiah and Christ. How? If, for example, the psalmist speaks about spiritual consolation, the source of that consolation naturally is the Messiah. If a person approached a prophet in the Old Testament and said, "You keep talking about our 'consolation,' but you haven't told us when we will receive it," the prophet would respond, "Have patience. It will be when the Messiah comes." Remember the statement, "I know that Messiah is coming. When He comes, He will tell us all things."[8] The source of all

---

8   John 4:25

knowledge and comfort in the Old Testament was the Messiah. So there could not be a psalm written without Christ being its focal point.

You might say to me, "Abba, you've made the Book of Psalms out to be a very big thing!" And I'll respond, "Absolutely—*absolutely so.*" The Psalter is like a spiritual father, or like a spiritual guide, teaching us every day. If the Psalms are written by the Holy Spirit, who can claim to be a spiritual father or guide in the Spirit's presence? And if the Spirit watches over you and feeds you, and provides you with a new "push" every day, as well as a new companionship—how blessed, how joyful are you!

The Psalms show forth your salvation in Christ with the utmost clarity. At one point, you might say, "My relationship with Christ is extraordinary," sensing delight in the sentiment that Christ is very near you. But then you err; and when you come to read the Psalms, you find each one closed off and locked in your face, with all the prior love having vanished. You will then approach a psalm with the plea, "Please, offer me something to drink. My throat is parched. How many times have I drunk from you! At least give me a single word to calm my heart." And the psalm responds, "No. Find another psalm." "My dear psalm, please! I've received so much from you." And it says, "No, not me today." And so, instead of praying (for example) "The Lord is my shepherd,"[9] which you once used to feed on so richly, and would pray while you walked before God as a white, spotless lamb, resting on Christ's shoulders—now the psalm refuses to answer you. You go to searching the other psalms, but nothing opens up to you except "Have mercy on me, O God, according to Your lovingkindness . . . wash me thoroughly from my iniquity,"[10] and the tears begin to fall.

One of the mysteries of the Psalms is God's search for the soul of man and His aim to renew its fellowship in Him by means of Christ.

9   Ps. 23
10 Ps. 51 (50 LXX)

It was for the sake of every man, or rather for the Church—which is the new Israel, obedient through the Person of Christ—that God endowed the Psalms with the Holy Spirit's voice, in order to eternally tie each person's soul to Himself. You will find this concept in *Orthodox Prayer Life*, where the angel blows the trumpet to call man to prayer. Prayer is a response, for nobody can stand before God in prayer without having responded to an initial divine call from within. The psalm, then, is the herald angel and the trumpet. You might say, "Very good. I won't pray unless God calls me to prayer by that trumpet." I will tell you that you misunderstood. Once you begin a psalm and detect the touch of the Spirit, you will know it to be an inward call to prayer, as well as permission from heaven to speak before God.

It's like Samuel.[11] He ran to Eli the priest and said, "Yes?" Eli asked, "What do you want, boy?" "Did you not call me?" "No." After several times, the old man realized the boy was being called by the Spirit. He told him, "My dear child, when you hear the voice, say, 'Speak, Lord, for your servant is listening.'" Samuel uttered those words, and the Lord proceeded to speak to him.

You might think, "I wish I were Samuel, or at least I wish I could have lived in his times; for then I would have witnessed such events and maybe even experienced them myself." I will tell you that what you have today is better than what Samuel had by a hundredfold. Every psalm is a call. Every psalm is an invitation to stand before God. If you read it properly, if you sing it properly, if you stand for prayer properly, if you open your mouth for praise with a humble and obedient heart, ready to accept God's voice—you will feel the call. Abbas, you will feel it. Really and truly, you will experience a divine call to speak in prayer, while the Lord hears all your petitions.

✛ ✛ ✛

---

11 1 Sam. 3

I want you to imagine with me for a moment a mental illustration of the praying man. My mind sees a certain brother standing in prayer while cords are being threaded and tied between him and the Lord. This brother leaves his cell while the cords are still connecting him to Christ, but he doesn't see them. The cords follow him everywhere. I ask him, "Come here, do you see that?" He asks, "What?" I tell him, "There are cords made of gold stretching out from your heart. Can't you see them?" "I see nothing." "Dear brother, there are golden cords there, and they have written on them the *iota*[12] —the name of Jesus! They go with you everywhere!" Whenever I stand before God and become immersed in the psalm, and speak to God as He speaks to me (these are not cheap words thrown around the air!), I receive the living and active Word of God. Heaven and earth and the body might pass away, but the Word that tied my heart to God will never pass away.

You might tell me dejectedly, "Abba, I've been in a very low spiritual state lately." I will answer, "Don't be afraid. The Lord is with you, and you have strength and life in you; they're just hidden from your eyes." You might then respond, "Abba, you always offer me a grand message of consolation, but it is really beyond me." I would say, "No, I'm confident of what I'm saying. I know your past life and how you've made real contact with God through your prayers. You've made genuine, spiritual contact with Him. And isn't it true that whatever God binds, no man can separate?[13] Not even the devil!" Prayer is contact. The Psalms are lines of communication. Each psalm is a heavenly ring that encircles me with Christ.

Praise and supplication are both means of contact, whether the praise of joy or the praise of sorrow. You might entreat God thus: "Until when, O Lord, will You forsake me? Where is Your word on

---

12   *Iota* is the first letter of the Greek name "Jesus": Ἰησοῦς.
13   Mark 10:9

which I've depended? My soul is eaten up by the dust. My eyes are consumed by tears. How long will You leave me?"

I'll say, "Ah, what wonderful praise is this!"

You will respond, "Praise? I'm complaining to God! I'm yelling and upbraiding Him."

I will say, "No, this is praise raised to the highest degree."

Praise does not just include words like, "Holy, holy, holy" and "Hallelujah" and "You who sit on the cherubim"—and all such beautiful phrases—but every complaint and groaning is also a form of praise. All types of such praise develop into cords that bind us to God, and one day the cords will be made plain to us. Every prayer we utter, hour by hour and day by day, is kept and recorded. I've told you many times before, and here I say it again, that everything you have can be stolen from you or lost—except your prayers. Whatever you offer up, whether in five minutes or an hour, will be *preserved forever*.

✟ ✟ ✟

The Psalms are given as a light to illuminate man's way to God and to reveal the salvation that binds him to God. "A lamp unto my feet, and a light unto my path." Do you open up an oil lamp and examine its parts in order to find out where you're going? Not at all. You grasp it and stretch out your hand in order to light up the way before you. Your approach to the Psalms should be the same. I'm afraid my profuse talk about the Psalms might cause you to dissect them laboriously in hopes of finding out the depths contained in them. But that's never my method in studying the Bible. God's Word is not closed, and the Holy Spirit is not in need of anyone to explain Him. That would be a tragedy. The Spirit is the one who explains everything to man; so if *He* required someone to explain *Him*, than woe to us!

Every psalm is a beautiful house for the Holy Spirit, and your duty is to stand quietly at the door. You will find the Spirit coming out to you with open arms, saying, "Welcome, my dear guest! My visitant of the day! Enter, enter, eat and drink with Me." The Psalms are thus simple and inviting, because they are written by the Holy Spirit. We might need to do a little study of the history and translation of each one in order to understand their general drift and message; but other than that, you won't need to exhaust your intellect in figuring out what God wants of you. All that is required is that your heart be *open* and *ready* as you read.

Again, reading a psalm is not a sort of mental exercise, requiring systems and rules to extract its meaning. It is rather a *gift*. And your nourishment from the gift is not a difficult thing, but you are required to make your way into the heart of the psalm. Let me give you an illustration. Imagine the psalm as a series of concentric rings: it's one very large ring, than a smaller one inside, then a yet smaller one inside, and so on until the center. The outer ring is the first level of interpretation, and each smaller ring gives you a deeper level of meaning. (However, the first verse is not necessarily the first ring but could be the second or third. I never like mere numbers to control our spiritual thinking.) At the center is the core meaning of the psalm's mystery.

I said before that Christ is the center of each psalm. Yes; but the mystery at the center also equates with the psalm's gift to you. It will *give* you humility, love, joy, comfort, vision, correction, zeal—it will give you an abundance of good things! But you must surrender yourself to the psalm from its very beginning, and it will lead you on to the center. If you try to dissect it verse by verse, you will not reach its depths. Surrender yourself. The psalm has a secret way of leading you. Each verse knows how to push you along deeper and deeper, until you meet the divine mystery at the center, along with the Spirit who is speaking to you.

But if you try to take the psalm by force, if you ask what this or that verse exactly means, you will end up being a mere interpreter, and it will be very difficult to receive your gift in that way. The *interpretation* of a psalm is one thing, and the *praise* of a psalm is something quite different. Again, interpreting a psalm is one thing, but offering it up to God liturgically is something else entirely. If you take the road of commentating on the Psalms and resorting to famous commentators, even Athanasius or Cyril the Great—the number of commentators on the Psalms is staggering—you might become a *scholar* of the Psalms, but not a *liturgist*. You will not be a servant of the Psalms; you will not be a *psalmist*. I am emphasizing the difference between exposition or interpretation on the one hand, and praise, doxology, and service on the other, because the former leads to mental understanding, whereas the latter leads to spiritual gifts.

✝ ✝ ✝

The Psalms draw for us a sharp picture of the grandeur and power of God, along with His love, compassion, and tender mercies. The collective participation of the Church in the Psalter's praises *unifies* the thoughts and feelings of the many separate individuals involved. We become a united body with a united purpose, which is to unite man to God. The language of some psalms rises to the most exquisite descriptions of God's nature. You see the psalmist rising higher and higher in his descriptions of God until he reaches a very lofty pinnacle; and the psalm has been recorded for the joy of all later generations. You pray the psalm and find yourself coming to me and saying, "I want to tell you about God!" I reply, "Tell me." You present your description, and I respond, "How amazing. Would you believe I read the same thing in Athanasius's works?" And you stare in awe.

Athanasius, by the way, was enthralled by the Psalms, and the same can be said generally of all the Church Fathers. There is not a single

Father for whom the Psalms were not a preeminent book that testi-fied to the relationship that bound them to Christ. The Fathers quote from them richly. This amount of preoccupation with the Psalms, I'm sad to say, has declined significantly today. The Fathers learned to place such an enormous value on the Psalms from their predecessors, who learned the same from the Apostles, who in turn learned so from Christ. When Christ desired to call upon a witness to Himself, He would quote from the Psalms. "The Lord said to My Lord . . ."[14] Ah, how beautiful are Your ways, O Lord, and with what fine felicity did You express such things regarding Yourself!

Athanasius lived in the fifth century, and you live in the twentieth; but if you live deeply in the Psalms, you will feel yourself closer to Athanasius in spirit and will better understand him. You might even say, "I almost feel myself become a theologian, Abba." I will respond that it's a very natural thing to happen to someone living with God in the Church. For who is the theologian? It's the person who sees God, and I mean spiritually sees Him. The theologian is the one who nurtures a relationship with God. But this definition has been turned on its head, for do you know what makes a "theologian" nowadays? It's the person who writes theological books; and he may even lead a prof-ligate life. "Is that possible?" you ask. Yes, it's possible; in the twentieth century, anything is possible. But in the early centuries, theology was service and life in God. The theologian developed his theology as the outflow of his personal life.

"I have understood something new today from your words, Abba," you might tell me. "The Church today is divided because it does not have a unified vision of God." I will respond, "Precisely. You have put your finger on the nose." If our hearts possessed a unified picture of God, we would unite in spirit, in opinion, in thought. You see now the source of that unity for which we so earnestly yearn? Its source is

---

14 Matt. 22:44

clearly in God. If you stand diligently before God in your prayers, and I do the same, our hearts will open up to each other (even in theological ideology), and God will be the bridge between us. Our thoughts, our feelings, our behavior, our goals, and everything else will be united in a bond of love.

Have you understood now that, in a monastic community, the Psalms are the primary force in the genesis of the union between us? And from my own experience, when a monk neglects his Psalms, his relations with God and his brethren wither, he turns sluggish in his spiritual rule, and he experiences an inner discord. He comes and complains that he is not in harmony with the community. He remarks that the other monks do not like him, while I know for certain that they really do. It is because their hearts are open to his, but his is closed up. The mystery, therefore, that unites us on earth is the same mystery that will unite us in heaven: God Himself. The Psalms give us the opportunity to taste that unity we will one day know in heaven.

The Power of the Psalms

1973

The Psalms as used in the Church assume as their starting point a few things: the worshipper's standing in God's presence by Christ's Spirit; his speaking to God by Christ's mouth; his supplicating God in Christ's name; and finally, his entering into the newly created relationship with God by virtue of the new relationship with Christ. I sing praises *with* Christ, sharing His same confidence; and by virtue of His eternal sacrifice, I assume the *boldness* of having Christ as my Mediator for the acceptance of my praise before the Father. "Whatever you ask in My name, that I will do."[1] He has thus given us His name as a mediatorial token; and, His tongue being equal to His name, it has also become a mediatorial token for offering up our praise to God. If I lift up prayers to God in Christ's *name*, then I do so by His *tongue* as well. Praise, therefore, grants us a very great measure of boldness before God. Since Christ prayed with the Psalms, this boldness has even become a canonical right. That

---

1   John 14:13

is, I have the "legal" privilege and right to stand before the Father in Christ, by Christ, and with Christ.

Considering all this, can I then say that the Psalms are limited in the Bible to that position after Job? Or before Proverbs? But I find them in Revelation, in the Gospels, and in the Epistles, and therefore I can't say that they are just an Old Testament book. The rest of the Old Testament books do belong in the Old Testament—but not the Psalms.

Christ prayed with the Psalms the night of the Last Supper. After they had eaten, they went up to the Mount of Olives, praying Psalm 118. It begins with "give thanks," that is, the *eucharist*; and it tells us to "bind the sacrifice with cords to the horns of the altar." A psalm so full of mystery! They praised as they walked out to Mount Olivet, and the Lord was the chorus leader. He would sing a praise, and they would utter the response. He constructed an actual liturgy out of the Psalms; but what can one possibly say of such a liturgy? It was more than an angelic liturgy, it was a wholly *divine* one! My goodness, to what heights of significance the Psalms have reached! After I had meditated upon Psalm 118, it transformed in my eyes into a psalm of divine ideas. It has become a formidable prayer to my mind, and I approach it with trembling.

✠ ✠ ✠

We must discover God's voice speaking in the Psalms, but the discovery cannot be made without Christ as its living and illuminating center. If a psalm's theme is thanksgiving, then Christ is the source of that thanks in the Eucharist. If the theme is supplication, then Christ is the source of the supplication with His arms outstretched on the Cross. The Psalms, remember, are not thrown together into a shapeless heap, but they are categorized by theme: thanksgiving, supplication, spontaneous praise, divine mystery, and so on. And there is not a psalm that does not have Christ as the source of its content or essence.

For example, the words, "Have mercy on me, O God, according to Your lovingkindness and according to the multitude of Your tender mercies,"[2] have no value without the Cross; the *mercy* here requested descends upon us only from the arms stretched out on the Cross. Can I offer a "new praise" except by the light of the Resurrection and its joy? Can any praise be "new" except in the name of the Lord Jesus? So I say, Christ has become the essence and ground-of-being for each psalm. Without Christ, the psalm is stripped of its authority and power and of its message to you.

I said before that we hear God's voice in the Psalms by the mediation of Christ when we discover Him as the living and illuminating center of the psalm; and by the light Christ shines, we also find ourselves in it. The psalm becomes our own, that is, our personal worship, the liturgy of our private lives, which we offer up every day to God. I thus offer the sacrifice of my own self—a portion of my life. "Let me be excused, Abba," you say to me. And I respond, "Where are you going?" "I'm going to offer my sacrifice." "A sacrifice? What type of sacrifice?" "I'm going to pray the psalms of the ninth hour." It's the sacrifice of praise, and it's pregnant with mystery. The sacrifice I am offering up is the content of my entire life, from the moment I was conceived in my mother's womb until this very hour.

And when I stand to pray with the Psalms, I'm not only offering up my own life, but also reviewing the redemptive history of Israel—which represents myself as well as the Church. In the Psalms I live the exodus, I live the passage through the Red Sea, and I live Christ on the Cross. Through these things I come to learn about my salvation. All the dealings of God with mankind are contained in the Psalms—and

---

2   Ps. 51:1

I pray them. They are the history of man's services offered to God and the history of God's mercies offered to man. I live this history of salvation and *participate* in it; and he who participates in salvation also contributes to *perfecting* it.

What kind of person do you think it is who never contributes to the salvation of the world? Simply the unsaved person. A follow-up question: Can a person live out his salvation without influencing the salvation of others? It's impossible. When I stand for prayer and work out my salvation from day to day, I am affecting the salvation of others as well as of the Church. Imagine if the Church had not had even one person who really lived out his salvation—could we say that such a Church possessed salvation? Imagine instead if each person in the Church lived out his salvation but partially. The Church would be filled with salvation! Do you see that when you live out your salvation—by attending diligently to your prayers and by your faithfulness in serving—you're nurturing your own soul while simultaneously filling the Church with salvation?

✠ ✠ ✠

If the Psalms form the basis for the liturgy in the New Testament, then they also help to reveal the work of the sacraments in us, as well as inducing sacramental power in us. There can be no Eucharist except that which concludes in praises that employ the Psalms. This is part of our tradition and not just a personal thought of my own. For example, our tradition forbids the serving of communion in church while some persons sit in the back mourning. I once entered into a sharp quarrel with a monk who became extremely upset at me. The church was partaking of Holy Communion while he was chanting a hymn in the paschal tone.[3] I told him, "Halt it."

---

3   The paschal tone in the Coptic Church, which is used only during

He said, "No, this is how it's supposed to be."

I said again, "Halt it. Our prayer says, 'My mouth is filled with joy and my tongue with exultation.'"[4] I can never tolerate chanting that is not joyful while the sacrifice is being offered.

It's also inappropriate for one to be gloomy or dejected after having received communion. It indicates that he did not receive it correctly. If you receive communion the right way and allow its effective working in you, you will barely be able to contain yourself for joy. You will not even be able to conceal your smile. You will leave church in a state of elation and excitement and rejoicing. You will cry out, "*Sotees*, amen!"[5] You might even be mistaken for a Protestant, exclaiming the word "saved!" with such enthusiasm. How unfortunate it is that these words are not said with more joy during the liturgy!

The praise that I offer up after receiving communion is simply the expression of the *effect* or *impact* the Eucharist has on me after having received it. If I therefore find someone mouthing the praises who hasn't partaken of the Eucharist, I'll naturally ask him, "What reason have you to be praising? If you want to praise rightly, come inside and partake of communion first." There was a time when monks used to skip communion in order to proceed straight to the podium in order to be the first to publicly raise their voices in singing. (But thank God this doesn't happen anymore. We are really in a time of grace these days, and there is a new spirit permeating all of us. God knows how much I feel the power and activity of the Holy Spirit working among us.) Such behavior will never work! Can you really be in a state of true

---

Holy Week, is characterized by a strong tinge of pathos or mourning and so is impossible to mix with any festive tone, especially during communion.

4   This is an individual prayer the Coptic faithful recite after partaking of Holy Communion.

5   An exclamation uttered several times throughout the Coptic liturgy which means, "Saved, Amen!"

joy without having received communion? The most beautiful praises I have ever heard were those chanted at the altar.

If the sacraments work in a person's life, the Psalms will work in his mouth. When a person says the Psalms are tasteless to him, I respond that he is still in need of baptism and needs to renounce Satan all over again! I greatly fear when a monk tells me the Psalms are tasteless to him. Again, the Psalms elucidate the effect the sacraments have on our souls, and they enable us to fully realize the extent of the sacramental power in us. A sacrament's power, in other words, is maximized through the Psalms. For example, if a monk comes and says to me, "Abba, when I partake of Holy Communion, I feel all aflame. I want to preserve this effect always!" I reply, "You can—through the Psalms. By engaging in exultant praises, you will never lose the power conveyed by the sacraments." These words are plain but mystical. You will hopefully feel the sense of what I'm saying because I can never exactly explain it.

✛ ✛ ✛

"Praise God in all His saints!"[6] What does this mean? It points to our *inheritance*: "the eyes of your understanding being enlightened, that you may know what is the hope of His calling, what are the riches of the glory of His inheritance in the saints."[7] There is an interpretation of the "inheritance of the saints" which perplexes me because it comes from several reputable commentators but reverses the true meaning. They say that Christ receives His inheritance in the saints. Rather, it means that *we can receive our inheritance only among the saints*. In other words, I must be personally standing among the ranks of the saints

6   Ps. 150:1, according to the Septuagint and Coptic versions, taking the Greek word ἁγίοις to mean *saints*. This is the first praise uttered during the reception of Holy Communion in the Coptic Church.
7   Eph. 1:18

to receive my portion of this inheritance in Christ. "There is no salvation outside the Church." So the phrase "Praise God in all His saints" means you cannot praise Him strictly alone. Such praise will not rise as a pleasing aroma of incense before God. But when you stand among the saints, with due respect for them and in consideration of them, everyone's praise is offered up together before God.

Every psalm is a stairway ascending to heaven. And it is also a descending stairway from God into your heart and the inner depths of your being. It changes and renews all that is decaying within you. In a moment, while you're standing in prayer, you suddenly feel yourself engulfed in flames. And that which you could not change in yourself, though you tried for a lifetime, will be changed in a moment without toil. The salvation we start to engage in praying with the Psalms—in strife and tears and patience—God finishes in the end by His own serene and comforting presence. We call the Paraclete the "Comforter": so we may ask, how does He comfort? By allowing us to feel our nearness to God, and by convincing us that our salvation is nearer to us than when we first believed.[8] The Spirit makes us feel that we are situated within God's love and mercy, and that we are surely on the high road to salvation.

✛ ✛ ✛

How often it happens that we stand to pray while tired, with ankles trembling, a body exhausted and failing, and nerves swollen—but nevertheless by striving to finish our prayers, we find in the end our soul and body in a fervent heat, with the desire to sit down having utterly abandoned us. And once we finally do sit, seeing the inflamed state that caught our soul, we become amazed at our initial reluctance to pray! Lord, give me a tongue to prick every lazy soul! Behind the

---

8   Rom. 13:11

laziness there is a kindling fire awaiting you, and the Spirit is waiting to aid you abundantly if only you persist.

We sow what we reap. Sometimes we pray the Psalms in tears. We come and moan, "We're too tired, Abba. There's no time. It's dark at night and you order us to turn the lights out. It's difficult to light a match and find the lamp." In tears, I say, we pray the Psalms. But oh, for the joy we find once the psalm is firmly planted in the heart! There's no plant in the world that can be planted and bear fruit in just two hours—only the Psalms.

Inasmuch as we persist in our struggle to pray, insomuch does God persist in pouring out His grace on us. Whenever we persist in prayer, in the absence of outward consolation and encouragement, God can never allow it to become a loss. Consider this a spiritual law: Inasmuch as you make it a *consistent rule* to struggle during prayer (even when tired), insomuch will you unknowingly cause the Spirit to make it a consistent rule to offer you consolation. His consistency will match your own.

The Holy Spirit is consistent in consoling us, in strengthening us, in encouraging us, and even in healing us. Many a time has a man begun prayer while physically sick and completed it with his health restored. I know a man who once received a vicious scorpion sting that swelled up his entire neck. (You know how dangerous neck stings can be, as they are so close to the brain.) He entered his room to pray and cried, "O Adversary of all goodness, will you indeed prevent me from praying?" He placed his hand over the swollen area and proceeded with his entire prayer regimen, and having finished, found not a trace of the sting left anywhere, not even of the original puncture wound.

We must approach prayer in a proper and erect posture. One should not pray cross-legged, or propped up against a wall, or leaning on a staff. If I would fall without a staff, then I must use it; but if I can go without it, then I should. One's posture during prayer ought to exhibit reverence, dignity, and a certain awe. The proper stance during prayer allows the latent message, or the latent Spirit rather, to be revealed to me. If one stands with a bit of carelessness, it will be impossible to progress.

I'm telling you this, Abbas, because you are my beloved, and I don't mean to scare you, or to burden you, or to intimidate you. But it is impossible for the Spirit to work in a man's heart if he's standing to pray beset by carelessness, resentment, or anger. His heart must be thoroughly cleaned up. When we greet each other with the *azpaseste*,[9] for example, in preparation for the Eucharist, it's a genuine azpaseste that we perform and not a mere jest or empty rite. I do not merely clasp my hands with my brother's in vain, but it is a true and holy kiss—by which I trample the enemy under my feet. There must be a total solidarity between me and my brother.

If you stand before God to pray while your heart is at peace with all people and free of bitterness, the Holy Spirit will absolutely come to you with comforts and blessings, and will cause you to grow day by day. Tell me, what causes a psalm to occasionally begin and end with no result? It's due to an attitude of lassitude, of laziness, of being propped up against a wall—but once the prayer is over, you become suddenly full of energy again. Why is it that as you're at prayer you feel slow and drained, shifting from one leg to the other, but once you're done, you go out and easily stand for an hour to chat with

9   Gr., "kiss." This is spoken by the deacon during the liturgy as a signal to the congregation to greet each other with the ancient Coptic greeting, i.e. a gentle mutual hand clasp between two believers, after which the folded hands are brought up to the lips as an emblem of the "kiss of peace." See Rom. 16:16.

your brother? Look, Abbas, the Fathers have taught that an attentive stance will lead to an attentive mind, and an attentive mind will lead to an awareness of the Spirit's work in us.

I will tell you what this is like. (Lord, give me wisdom.) It's like a light bulb that refuses to function, and I ask Abba Silvanus to go investigate. He returns and says the wattage is wrong—the bulb is 110 volts, while our outlet is equipped for 220 volts. I may ask Abba Silvanus, "What's so important about wattage?" and he will respond that it's what provides the power for the bulb to light. So when the bulb's wattage is incorrect, the power provided is dissipated and lost. The wires in the bulb then become frayed and useless.

Sin, likewise, eats up the wires of the heart; or, alternatively, when the soul is fattened through excessive eating, the heart's wiring is also fattened, so the power provided is not conducted properly and gets wasted. The light doesn't come on. Exactly so, beloved, does the mysterious work of the Holy Spirit proceed inside the heart of man. If a man's heart is equipped to properly conduct the power provided by the Holy Spirit, he will give off light and warmth. But if his heart is not adapted to the Spirit's power level, how will that man receive anything? The power is being fed into the bulb, but the bulb doesn't light. You might say the problem is in the generator, but I will respond that the generator is functioning just fine, because if you place your finger into its power source, you'll receive a shock. The bulb simply does not have the same wattage as the power source.

This is not merely a simplified analogy but actual doctrine. If you want it stated in simpler terms, I will tell you that you must stand for prayer attentively, with a clean and alert heart, and a soul at peace with the whole of creation. St. Isaac the Syrian says a person must be at peace with every creature crawling upon the face of the earth. There shouldn't even be the least hostility between you and an insect. Enmity between us and any part of creation causes a blockage in the power flow to our light bulb. Give it a try: If you stand for prayer one day and are harassed by a fly, reach out and crush it; then see if you can continue prayer. Your rage at the fly will strip your prayer of its vitality. Strange thing! But when the heart, mind, and body are all in a state of vigilance, the Holy Spirit's work finds no obstacle in its way. Such an obstacle would be quite impossible. You *will* feel the action of the Holy Spirit within you; and you will rejoice in it, and you will proclaim it abroad.

✠ ✠ ✠

Again, we must realize that the Psalms together do not merely make up an Old Testament book, but they are the reflection of God's dealings with mankind throughout all generations. And they are thus found quoted throughout the entire Bible. Psalms is truly a book without boundaries. The Spirit brought them together into a focused collection of prayers, supplications, and praises. Having realized this, it becomes one of our chief duties to pay the closest attention to the words and message of the Psalms, as well as to bring the Psalms to bear on our studies of the rest of the Bible.

One of the things that made the Psalms particularly attractive to me was their connection to so many of the other biblical books. But to the person who lacks an intimate familiarity with the rest of the biblical books, the Psalms will appear quite limited in scope. To fully grasp the depth and breadth of the Psalms, you must study them side by side with the other books. If you own a Bible with references, follow each one and see where it takes you. That way you will discover those connections by the easiest means possible. I would never advise a new monk to use a Bible without references, because without their help you are wasting your days and years and expending immense amounts of effort in vain. When you begin to understand where each Psalm originated and what is its aim, the Psalter will increase in weight and value in your eyes.

Find your place in each psalm. Instead of referring the Psalms back to historical events in the Bible, you must refer them directly to yourself, so that they may inform particular events in your life and you may be elevated higher. I should give you several examples of this, but since we will be studying the Psalms individually in detail later, we will content ourselves now with this introductory summary.

I am offering these basic guidelines to the Psalms by which your hearts might have joy and your souls might find nourishment; this is what primarily concerns me. As I have said before, I am neither a preacher nor a professor. I am simply a traveler on the road, pointing out the steps I have trodden and saying, "Come, let's go together and walk upon the way the Fathers have shown us."

The spiritual walk has become scarce these days. In the days before Malachi, it was said that "the word of the Lord was precious in those days."[10] However, the word of the Lord is no longer scarce these days. Biblical knowledge and teaching has swollen to an absurd size; every and any person now can teach and write commentaries. But where is the *walk*? Do we adapt our steps to those of Christ and walk along the divine path? *This* is what is "precious" in our days.

I pray that God would give us many calm and peaceful years, and that He would give me strength to repeat gatherings like this. Put these words into your hearts and transform them into prayer, that you may be more attentive to your salvation, that we may be more attentive to our common mission, and that we may grow in love for one another.

---

10 1 Sam. 3:1. "Precious" in the same way a stone is precious, that is, because of its scarcity.

The Value of the Psalms

1973

Brethren, let us continue our contemplation of the Psalms. There is an idea abroad among those who like to contemplate only with their brains,[1] and who are accustomed to the criticism of spiritual things and patristic teaching, to which we must respond. I must mention this idea here in our discussion in order to relieve your constantly restless minds. It's the notion that, since the Psalms are contained in the Old Testament canon, it's unreasonable to make them a real part of our New Testament experience. But the Old Testament will remain "old" only as long as it is read apart from Christ. After we have known Christ, we no longer see it in the old light. It remains old to others (such as the Jews who have not yet received Christ), and no longer has any relevancy to the modern world. But when Christ, the fulfillment of Old Testament symbolism, was revealed, the symbol itself changed from an old life to something living and new.

When the disciples walked with our Lord on earth, their questions

---

1   As opposed to "thinking" with one's heart or one's faith.

about the Kingdom made it clear they didn't understand the true meaning of God's salvation. In Old Testament times, the people of Israel conceived of salvation as a narrative that unfolds in time here on earth. When they crossed the Red Sea, for example, the whole people sang that magnificent praise.[2] They had just reached Sinai's shore when Miriam the sister of Moses took the cymbals in her hands and began singing and dancing. It was not a measured and balanced hymn, but it is nevertheless one of the greatest praises in the entire Bible. The people lifted up this praise merely because they had reached Sinai, because "salvation" to them meant release from slavery; yet the concepts of a spiritual salvation and an eternal life with God were alien to them. Then, when Christ came to reveal these things to them, they were unable to comprehend it, and they preferred to remain in their earthly mode of thinking. They refused to believe in a spiritual form of salvation.

This should not be our state today. Just this morning we sang the praise of Moses with joy.[3] Our joy might be somewhat less than theirs was on that day, because they were dancing with the timbrel in their hands; but we praise with spiritual insight. The essence of salvation in the Old and New Testaments is essentially the same, because it is Christ Himself. You remember what St. Paul said, "For they drank of that spiritual Rock that followed them, and that Rock was Christ."[4] The rock was to them a desperate form of salvation, but merely on the level of drinking, because they were dying of thirst. This shows us the pettiness of man, Abbas, that just for the sake of a bit of

---

2   Ex. 15
3   The monastic rite in most Coptic monasteries includes the recital of the praise of Moses in the Coptic language during the early hours of the day.
4   1 Cor. 10:4, an allusion to the story in Exodus 17, where Moses struck his rod against a rock in obedience to God's command, which resulted in the miraculous provision of water for the people.

water he sings and dances and appoints a yearly feast for the event.

But when we have learnt the spiritual significance of it all—that the rock was Christ; that "whoever drinks of the water that I shall give him will never thirst;"[5] that he will not only drink of the water but will himself become a fountain of life-giving water—despite these great mysteries, we are not moved to dance as the people of Israel danced of old. And when we happen to see another monk a little too emphatic or zealous in his praising, we murmur and say to ourselves, "Why is he so emotional?" Well, why don't you first search into the secrets of the salvation you've been given? When Miriam uttered her praise, it was not about someone else, but it emanated directly from her own spirit to God.

The contrast I'm drawing between us and Israel is really a sad one. Israel cries out in joy for the sake of a physical deliverance (and what exquisite compositions they made!), then they hand them on to us and say, "Take this from us, O following generations, and pray in the spirit"—yet we can't even rise to their level! Can anything reveal our feebleness more than this? I'm trying to demonstrate for you how feeble the Church has become.

But it was not always so. The Church[6] was originally soaked in psalmody. Think of St. Mary's praise: "My soul magnifies the Lord, / And my spirit has rejoiced in God my Savior."[7] This is an ordered, balanced psalm in the original Hebrew, which she uttered by the Spirit. And Zechariah's praise[8] was also a psalm uttered by the Spirit. These and similar prayers are all psalms. And it's incorrect, by the way, to say that we have only one hundred and fifty psalms. We are cheating ourselves. You have to add in the *Magnifcat*, the *Benedictus*, and

---

5 John 4:13
6 The Old Testament church is here included.
7 Luke 1:46, 47
8 Luke 1:67–79

the first chapter of the Gospel of John. There are very few people who recognize that John 1 is both a poem and a psalm. Listen:

> *In the beginning was the Word,*
> *And the Word was with God.*
> *The Word was God,*
> *He was in the beginning with God.*
> *All things were made through Him,*
> *And without Him nothing was made that was made.*
> *In Him was life,*
> *And the life was the light of men.*
> *The light shines in the darkness,*
> *But the darkness did not comprehend it.*

You see the poetry? And this is just in translation. When you go back to the original Greek, the poetic element becomes even clearer. When you go the Book of Revelation, you will find at least twenty to thirty different psalms.

Forgive me for saying this again, but we monks today not only fail to use the Psalms properly, but we even grumble that they are hard to comprehend. "I can't understand them, Abba, and I don't see the beauty in them." We can't even achieve the materialistic level of joy Israel experienced on the day of their physical deliverance, though we are given more—eternal salvation, as well as the Blood that cleanses us. This is bestowed on me even in the teeth of my stubborn will.

Do you remember when a mother used to come at the end of the week and usher all the children into the bathroom to be washed? They probably don't do it anymore these days, but the child who attempted to escape the wash would receive a good spanking. The mother would seize him and force him to be washed, even amid his protests and screaming. In my mind, I imagine the Holy Spirit does the same with us. He took us into the baptismal font to be washed in the eternal waters—even as we screamed—and throughout later life, he continues to cleanse and purge and correct us amidst our screaming.

So I say, we who live in the era of the Holy Spirit fail to appreciate the Psalms. The Church should be eternally speaking and reverberating the Psalms. I cannot say the Church should be *composing* psalms, because they were not designed on any method. They were spontaneously created by a surge of the Spirit on the spur of the moment, and that is why they are not strictly regular and do not rhyme. Nevertheless they do have a lyrical or musical flow to them. Our Church has even adopted this method in the construction of her Coptic hymns.

This spontaneity also used to apply to the words of the eucharistic prayer.[9] Today the priest must memorize it to the letter, but back then it was never memorized. Not only that, but it was not even written down. Not only that, but it was never said the same way twice! The bishop used to stand and freely utter whatever the Spirit gave him at the moment to pray over the Eucharist. But with time, a certain number of the most eloquent and spiritual eucharistic prayers were collected and put down as the official prayer. The process was somewhat akin to the way the Psalms were compiled into one book. That is, prayers were once freely offered up in the Spirit; but when the communication between man and the Spirit slowed, we needed to draw on the treasures of our ancestors and renew them for our own use.

If a man utters the words of his praises in all sincerity, his spirit will rise. You must pay close attention to the words you are saying; and what's more, you ought to be adding words from your own heart. This applies mostly to your prayers while alone in your cell. After you

---

9 By "eucharistic prayer" Abba Matta refers to what the Coptic liturgical books in America term the "Institution Narrative." The priest recites a paraphrase of the words Christ spoke at the Last Supper for the consecration of the oblation.

sing a written verse, respond to it with a verse of your own making, because this will be a concrete expression of the bursting-out your soul feels. It's said of St. Macarius that there was a pathway that led to his cell, and as he walked it he would recite twenty-five prayers composed by himself. His prayers, as St. Augustine says, were like arrows that shot straight upward to heaven. They were also arrows that pierced and burned the devil. You see how the Church and her monks used to live out the Psalms every day. And here we are now, at the end of the ages, just starting to learn what the Book of Psalms is all about!

I think by now we should be embarrassed to call the Psalms an "Old Testament" book. God's Word does not become exhausted or grow old. God's great scheme of salvation encompasses all the biblical books, new and old, and His methods far surpass man's expectation and vision. In the Book of Hebrews, St. Paul gives us glimpses of the Old Testament Scriptures and reveals how they are transformed into New Testament truth. He speaks about the sacrifices, about the blood, about the priesthood, about the constant mortality of the high priests compared with the immortality of our one High Priest, and practically turns the entire Old Testament into a New Testament book. Whoever lacks a taste for the Old Testament or thinks he can't understand it should read Hebrews.

A person once asked me, "Can you tell me the secret of becoming a saint? Or the secret to living always in God's presence?" I told him I would provide an extremely simple response, but he would have to think carefully about it in order to understand its depth. I said, "The secret to saintliness is a constant preference for God over everything else." A preference for God! In every situation where man finds himself, there is this tension: God versus the world; the Spirit versus the flesh; life according to God versus life according to this age. The two are always in conflict. So the secret to a saintly life comes down to this: Which side will you prefer and choose? It can't be once this way and once that way. You can't prefer the right way, then next time prefer the wrong, stumble and fall on your face, and expect to grasp the secret to saintliness. Rather, it is a pledge, a covenant—involving the greatest inward struggle—to always prefer God's way, no matter what the cost. Even death. *Here* is the secret to God's presence.

Every inclination we have to pray the Psalms is a chance to enter God's presence. The one requirement is the removal of the veil that covered Israel's eyes and hindered them from their God,[10] and which also hinders us. What was that veil that covered Israel's eyes other than a preference for material things? They loved money, possessions, authority, fame—all of these earthly things dominated their desires more than spiritual principles. Both their weddings and funerals were long, showy exhibitions. They had a continual leaning toward the flesh. Even their dealings with God took on a materialistic form; they would run to Him for increased money, for more children, for success in an enterprise. If such a veil would just fall from our eyes, the Psalms would become to us strains of heavenly music on which the spirit can soar.

You will tell me, "Okay, Abba, your words sound very nice. Now please give me an illustration by which I may fully understand you." Here it is: If a priest were to go up during the liturgy and read the Gospel without first reading the psalm, what would be the result?[11] The entire choir of deacons would storm him and insist that the psalm be read first. If the priest said, "Regardless, I'm starting directly with the Gospel," they would respond, "There can be no Gospel without the psalm first!" The psalm serves as a royal march chorus to introduce the King, because Christ is mystically revealed to us in the

---

10   2 Cor. 3:14–16

11   In the Coptic liturgy, a psalm is read directly prior to the Gospel, serving as a prophetic and lyrical groundwork for the Gospel's words. The psalm/Gospel reading is viewed as a single liturgical unit.

Psalms; and directly after the psalm is chanted, the priest utters the messianic announcement, "Blessed is He who comes in the name of the Lord!" It's all in line with the psalm that says, "Be lifted up, you everlasting doors, and the King of glory shall come in!"[12]

You see now how the knot that ties the Psalms and the Gospel together is extremely tight. The early Church assigned to the Psalms the first place among the biblical books that foretold Christ. When you read the Fathers who spoke about Christ's birth—whether Athanasius, Cyril, or any other—you will find that three-fourths of the prophetic Scriptures they quote are from the Psalter.

The Psalter is a book that requires of the reader or of the worshipper a spirit of *dedication*. Dedication! "Knock, and it will be opened to you."[13] Against what type of door are we knocking? The door of One who is good, full of mercy, and who will never refuse to open. It's a door of grace. It's a door that can never remain shut to the true supplicant. This is according to my own experience. There was never once in my life (O God, hear my confession) that I came to a verse in the Bible that puzzled me, desiring to receive blessing and grace, and it was not eventually revealed to me through steady persistence. Oppositely, the man who comes to the Bible with a careless and apathetic mind, who rushes through the Psalms without serious reflection, will reap very sparingly.

I say again that the quality of our commerce with the Psalms will not be determined by how scholarly or clever we are, but by the tone of our heart's relationship with the Lord. If there happens to be any knowledge that can be of service, I utilize it, mainly to provide a wider field in which our hearts can roam. Knowledge and research by themselves do not benefit us in anything; but a cleansed heart, tightly bound to Christ, is our treasure. There was never a time when

12 Ps. 24:7
13 Luke 11:9

I was torn and unsettled by discord and could still feel the Spirit's work. There was never a time that I felt distant from the Spirit and could still grow in virtue. Even if I found myself in the most profound depths of contemplation, the moment I became angry or perturbed at someone else, my spiritual vision would halt and I would find myself unable to write a word or meditate on anything. I would close the book before me and surrender myself to God. My *mind* would still be present, my *intelligence* would remain intact, but the *Spirit* would be silenced.

We have then no excuse for turning our backs on God. Have you ever known a friend who was a man of refined manners, of a sweet amiability, of cultured thinking, a gentleman and scholar? You would pay him the highest regard. You would greatly esteem such a friendship and consider him a companion of exceedingly great worth. Your interactions with him would exude the utmost respect. And if, one day, you did him a wrong turn or spoke a word slightly out of place and detected a look of displeasure on his face, you would quickly repent of your folly and vow never to make such a mistake again. Beloved, the same holds true for our dealings with the Spirit. The Spirit requires a certain standard of relationship. He requires that we realize the great value of this fellowship, realize the submissiveness and obedience needed from us, the constant confession of wrongdoing and perpetual repentance. Otherwise, *we* will be the losers. Our loss will be immense, and we will be without excuse.

I say we ought also to understand the high value of our relationship with the Psalms. It will not be determined by how many of them we've memorized, or how many commentaries we've read about them, but instead by the constancy of our dealings with them day and night. It's quite impossible that a person could pray a given psalm over and over and not receive some blessing from it; his efforts need only be thorough and sincere.

Let me repeat that the Psalms are not for the apathetic but for the person ready to take them seriously. Are we ready? Is it too much for us? You are able, in a moment's time, to plumb their depths with the Spirit, as long as you disengage from your old life and your old way of thinking, and kneel before God, saying, "I want to make a new beginning." This is, in fact, for the person who is just starting. As for the one seasoned and experienced in the way, he receives a stricter chastisement.

I want to make you aware of this, by the way. When a person starts his relationship with God, things go rather smoothly. But when he has been walking on the path for a while, if he makes a mistake, he will receive a good lashing. Believe it. Don't think life is easy and indulgent for the person who receives a plentitude of spiritual gifts. He who is given much, of him will be required *the more*.[14] On the other hand, the Spirit is meek and gentle with the wavering soul, with the poor sinner prostrate in compunction before the face of God. Before he even finishes his prostration, the Father embraces him. Before he weeps, the Father wipes his tears. Before he makes a request, the Father gives him more than he asks.

---

14   Luke 12:48

The Sinful Woman

1973

All of those who pray the midnight hour are familiar with this Gospel,[1] and it is possible that due to the constant frequency with which we come across it, it has lost much of its luster. I considered it beneficial therefore for us to contemplate it together, that our prayers might have some life in them. My attention has been drawn, in the first place, to the meticulous detail with which the supper is described. There are certain unspoken and implied details in the story that will astonish us, thrill us, penetrate us, and become pieces of our lives.

Let's cover the ritualistic aspect of this event first. We read, "And Jesus answered and said to him, 'Simon, I have something to say to you.' So he said, 'Teacher, say it.'" The Lord proceeds to tell a parable, then upbraids the Pharisee for neglecting a common hospitality: "I entered

---

1   Luke 7:36–50. The "midnight hour" in the Coptic canon is composed of three "watches," each of which features its own Gospel reading and litanies. The Gospel here in question refers to the second watch.

your house and you gave Me no water for My feet." Foot-washing was a common and essential service provided at Jewish meals. We lack the time to enter into a full explanation of the complexities that made up a Hebrew dinner, but dining in ancient Jewish culture was a sacred activity. In order to sit together at meal, a Jewish family would have to be in a state of prayer. And especially during large dinner-feasts, the rites of eating would take on an even more elaborate form.

We read further, "You gave Me no water for My feet, but she has washed My feet with her tears and wiped them with the hair of her head." This wiping with the hair of her head was not just an after-thought. It points us forward to Covenant Thursday, when the Lord washed the feet of the disciples, as well as to our Liturgy of the Water, where the priest washes the feet of the congregation. Again: "You gave Me no kiss, but this woman has not ceased to kiss My feet since the time I came in." Remember that when the deacon announces the kiss of peace, it signals the start of the liturgy.[2] Before the Jews would sit down to eat, they would exchange a kiss. The kiss was essential because it indicated the unity that bound those sitting at the dinner table, as did also the oneness of the loaf of bread they would break and share. You see, I'm drawing you away from the idea of a regular supper to that of a *mystical* one.

In these statements, Christ is making a sharp assessment of Simon's actions. He is saying, in effect, "You offered the kiss to the

---

2   The Coptic liturgy is divided into two primary sections. The first is the "Liturgy of the Word," which includes introductory prayers and Scripture reading; the second is the "Liturgy of the Faithful," which can be considered the liturgy proper, because it includes all the historical prayers of consecration and communion shared by other Orthodox liturgies. The "kiss of peace" is announced by the altar deacon at the start of the Liturgy of the Faithful, and it consists of a gentle clasping of the hands of every person within reach, which are then brought together to the lips as an indication of the kiss.

distinguished guests who entered your house but denied it to Me. Why? Is it because I am poor? Because I lack a luxurious garment? Because my sandals are not richly ornamented like those of important men? I came to your house at your own invitation, but you have withheld from Me the *kiss*." Christ is reproving the Pharisee for his indiscretion, and we will soon see why this Pharisee acted thus. "But this woman has not ceased to kiss My feet since the time I came in." Here the woman, in contrast, rises far above the Jewish traditions of her day. This is what is required *of us* too: "For I say to you, that unless your righteousness exceeds the righteousness of the scribes and Pharisees, you will by no means enter the kingdom of heaven."[3] This is why, at the end of the episode, the woman hears the words, "Your faith has saved you. Go in peace."

The woman's tears did not go unnoticed by Christ, as neither did the Pharisee's coldness go unnoticed. Both drew consequences. Christ is directing our attention here—by that characteristic touch both tender and strong—to the importance of the rite of the holy kiss. This practice is disregarded in the Church today; believers no more greet each other with the kiss. Even the momentary kiss exchanged during the liturgy has become an empty external act. But the kiss in its original form was an expression of the complete submission of one person's soul to another's.

The spiritual message of this Gospel is extremely deep, and we likely read it every day without gaining any benefit from a single line. No one these days is willing to exhaust his time and energy in harvesting from the Gospels what Christ meant to give us. The fact is that Christ is offering in this Gospel a clear model for two types of people: firstly the Pharisee, to whom was dealt a rebuke; and secondly the repentant woman, to whom was given salvation. This Gospel is, in fact, foundational for the building of the soul. Don't forget that we

3   Matt. 5:20

are in the month of Tute,[4] that is, the beginning of the year; and so the Church by her inspiration starts the year by giving us the lessons that are fundamental to the edification of the soul. She gives us (by the hand of St. Luke) a fundamental lesson couched in a story that is most beautiful and most vivid—you can even visualize the chamber in which our Lord and the guests sat. St. Luke pictures the whole scene for us with the two foremost personalities representing basic spiritual elements: guilt and repentance. In other words, Christ presents to us the *mystery of sin* embodied in the figure of the hypocritical Pharisee, and the *mystery of salvation* embodied in the figure of the penitent woman. And He tells us, "Choose."

There was one statement made that we can take as a key for contemplation in our spiritual life, which, at first glance, might not have seemed too important. Christ told Simon, "She was forgiven much, for she loved much." The idea seems at first to be stated backwards. It was not that she received forgiveness first, then began to love; but she loved first, then was forgiven. Christ's way of seeing things is different from man's. The love the woman offered was submitted under the cloak of repentance, and the people didn't recognize it. The meek and humble man does not seem to others like a person full of love, but in God's sight, he is a sincerely loving soul. What I want you to understand, Abbas, is that the source from which sprang all her courage and activity, which led her to salvation, was *love*.

Do you suppose there was found a trace of love in the Pharisee's heart? None. For you must understand what a Pharisee was. He exemplified the summit of religiosity. He was a man who observed all the traditions and ceremonies of his religion; he was trained in ecclesiastical usages, learned in the Scriptures, and a teacher among the people. Now, this great and revered teacher thrusts himself out

---

4   The first of the thirteen months that comprise the ancient Coptic calendar.

of God's favor in the story. He is judged and rebuked to the utmost degree. Why? Because he turned his religion into a source of blame.

This is the point I am trying to drive home. When religion is found devoid of love, it breeds pride and judgment. The Pharisee indignantly asked how the woman entered his house, how she dared to touch Christ, and how He would allow her to do so if He were a true prophet. Behold what religion becomes without love! It generates the evil eye. He looks at her and immediately knows her to be a sinful woman. But this also raises doubts about the Pharisee himself: How did he know about her sin? His eyes, heart, and soul all prove themselves to be distorted; thus, his judgment is a mere sham.

I can't say the woman was herself "religious." Her only credential was a love planted deep in her heart that could in no way be expressed in a religious way. But when her love finally reached Christ and was manifested to Him, it produced in her religion; and it was religion of a very high degree. This woman knew nothing of tradition or worship; but the love in her heart brought to her mind the name of Christ— that loving and righteous Teacher who was a friend of tax collectors and sinners—and when she heard that He was in the house of Simon the Pharisee, she resolved to approach Him and prostrate herself at His feet. Little did she know that deed itself was to be a wonderful type of worship. The Church seized on this act and made it an essential part of its prayers. As you know, our midnight prayer officially begins the new day, and so we start each morning with the lofty example of this woman's worship. As for the Pharisee, his position and knowledge of the law availed him nothing but a rejected piety.

This is a powerful warning to us as monks and servants. When love is mingled with repentance, we will hear the words, "Your sins are forgiven you." And when they murmured against this, the Lord added this: "Your faith has saved you." Where is this faith today, O Lord? When the woman's faith sought Christ, it filled her with the courage and persistence needed to approach Him. I say *persistence*, because there must have been a porter stationed at the door who attempted to bar her entrance. The love and courage in her heart that clung to the name of Christ engendered *faith*.

This is an astonishing thing, beloved! Many of you ask me, "How can we strengthen our faith?" Well, can you find in this sinful woman a model for its increase? When love seeks Christ's name, it sheds its fear and is made capable of bold deeds. A Pharisee's house was abhorrent to sinners, because it was strictly forbidden for a Pharisee to come into contact with a sinful woman. He would never dare make contact with her; and if they took to hitting her and forcibly casting her out, it would have been considered a laudable thing. The proper Pharisaic rules indicated that his duty was to afflict and expel her in order to avoid the risk of her polluting touch. But the woman paid absolutely no heed to any of these Pharisaic policies. She went in boldly and knelt at Christ's feet. She cried profusely, and anointed Him profusely, and wiped Him with her very hair.

All I can say is that this is precisely what Christ wants of us. He desires this large yet silent love of the sinful woman. Her shameful public acts, as well as her sordid history, were incapable of becoming barriers to her heart swelling with love for God. This is a beautiful fact, and it is also a message of encouragement to every sinner among us this morning. She comes, despite an appalling reputation but in a spirit of courage, and proves that love can be expressed as an act of repentance. She sought Christ, so that no obstacle could stand in her way, and neither was the Pharisee's door able to shut her out. Hers was a fervent and active love!

What should I say, Lord? Keep the door of Your house open to us! Never let it be closed to us on account of our weakness and fear. We have in this woman a calm and convincing proof that sin cannot stand in love's way. I can *run* to church—not merely walk or limp, due to feelings of unworthiness—and enter with my head uplifted in a spirit of confidence, knowing that Christ will accept me as He accepted the woman. Let us enter church, not distracted by the people moving around us but focused on our own hearts, which have been wrung by sin, and humbly kneel with the rest of the true worshippers.

Oh, that we would have the heart of the sinful woman! Lord, grant us a sense of the weight of our own sin. O woman, what is this that you have done? Did you touch the Savior's feet with your unclean mouth? Did you touch the holy Body with your sinful lips? O woman, you have opened a new door for us today! O sister, our habit is to distance ourselves from Him when we feel immersed in sin—we keep back to the section of the penitents.[5] Sometimes we don't even feel worthy to stand in the back area, but rather we stand completely outside the church. And why approach the church at all? I'm a sinner and ought to just stay at home.

But no! This isn't the teaching of the Gospel this morning. It doesn't sanction the different sections or boundaries or obstacles placed in the sinner's way. We learn, instead, how Christ's heart opens up to the sinner's heart with no intervening veil. We learn how the Lord offers His feet, as He calmly and happily awaits our approach. That very Body did not come to earth, brethren, other than for the sake of such unclean lips to kiss Him freely. If Christ were to come today, we would lift Him high up in an ivory tower, surrounded by all sorts of golden barriers, so that people would have to gaze from afar off to see Him. But no, He came down for the sake of being touched by—not clean, but unclean—lips, for the sake of every heart burdened by sin, and every eye wearied by transgression, that large tears might be shed upon that holy Body.

---

5   The early Church reserved an area toward the back of the church especially for those who were in a state of penance after having committed a "significant" sin.

Beloved, today a door of salvation has been opened to us, and it can never be shut by sin—no matter how ugly, or heavy, or disfigured, or terrible it may be. This door is Christ's forgiveness. It's the compassion gleaming in His eyes as He looks at the poor woman with joy, with love, and with tenderness. It's the smile that crossed our Lord's face, which offended and revolted the Pharisee. The Lord saw in the woman the form of the entire Church, which would come to Him in sin, weep on His feet, beg forgiveness, kiss the pure Body, and eat of it, too.

Who of you, brethren, have committed sins as great as this woman's? Perhaps none of you. But the Gospel offers us through her a model of repentance as great as that of the right-hand thief. You might say, "If I had lived in the days of the sinful woman, I would have acted the same way she did." My beloved, Christ is the same yesterday, today, and forever! Some complain to me, "Abba, I never weep. My eyes are hard and dry as rock." If you cannot weep over the Body, then eat it. When the priest places the holy Body in your mouth, say to Christ, "Lord, today I am a member in You. Consider me now to be like the sinful woman, kissing Your feet. I have partaken of You that You might cleanse me."

"To whom little is forgiven, the same loves little." Beloved, if your love is little, know that it's because your forgiveness is little, whereas your sin is big. There are many believers—the majority actually—who complain that the love among them is weak. Love is weak because sin is large, and the portion that is forgiven is small. Have you ever met a person on the verge of madness for the desire to serve and love others? He goes to the priest and announces, "Send me into any work that is needed. I'm willing to serve in any way possible! Whatever need comes to your mind, even be it at the edge of the world, *send me.*" This is a person who has abundant love, and it's because he received abundant forgiveness.

Have you understood now, beloved, that mysterious link that binds forgiveness to love? It's the mystery hidden in today's Gospel. Who here noticed this sacred bond upon reading this passage in the past? But we are too thoughtless! "To whom little is forgiven, the same loves little." These things are written for us, brethren. Forget about the Pharisee to whom it was spoken, who sought neither much nor little forgiveness. Christ directs these words at us.

My question to you, friend, is this: *Do you love much?* Do you exceedingly love Christ? You might say, "Explain." Many come to me and say, "Abba, my mind flees during prayer. I can finish an entire series of prayers, then realize I hadn't paid attention for a moment." Is this *much love?* Would you like to know what the thermometer of divine love is? Could you ever meet someone you love intensely and think about something else while you are talking to him?

Beloved, we must evaluate ourselves. If our mind is flighty during prayer, it means our love thermometer is reading a very low temperature. We are cold. The heart is not keeping up a warm pulse. If a physician takes a patient's temperature and finds it far below normal, he will check his heart, then order the nurse to fetch warming blankets for him. The spiritual father does the same. If he finds his son's prayers and exercise lagging, he urges him on to greater efforts, before his spiritual circulation becomes sluggish and his soul petrifies into a state of unchanging emptiness.

But you know, brethren, that at the end of days the love of many will grow cold, because "lawlessness will abound."[6] Be on guard, beloved. Sin ties up the mind; it chains one's soul and conscience. Do you think sin includes just filth and fornication? No, if you weigh pride and self-conceit, these are more pernicious than everything else. If sin makes its home in a person's bones and becomes a parasite in his soul and mind, his temperature drops, and forgiveness and love

---

6   Matt. 24:12

become strangers. People often ask me how we can increase the love between us: by running to God to confess our sins! Once we receive forgiveness, the love of God grows within us. But if a person does not love God, you know he's not throwing his sins upon Him. There is therefore no forgiveness, just guilt without love.

There is no other road to the love of God, brethren, except by the free casting of our sins before Him, in tears. Where do you suppose the sinful woman went after her encounter with Christ? She doubtless went straight to a house of worship. What did she buy in place of the cruse of oil? She doubtless purchased a Bible. How did she spend her nights instead of those lewd nocturnal practices? She spent them in the study of the Word. When forgiveness generates love, love generates worship.

I want to remind you of the man who absolutely refused a relationship with God. He used to say, "What God? And what's the use of church? These monks and priests are just a bunch of cheats who deceive the people to get their money." His heart was cold as stone. Then after some time, he needed forgiveness and was found praying in church. He once despised church, but now he stays after everyone else has left, beating his chest in repentance. You see what love does to you?

Some of you occasionally ask me why you care so little for church and are constantly in a hurry to finish your prayers. Your worship is weak because your love is weak; your love is weak because your forgiveness is absent; forgiveness is absent because sin still lurks in the crevices of your heart, and no one is searching it out. I am not sermonizing to you, my beloved; I am merely laying down the principles that ought to govern your lives. I am no preacher; I merely point out where your life has been and where it's going. I am showing you where you stand on the spectrum between the Pharisee and the sinful woman.

I want to say finally that love is *essential*. Humility, for instance, without love, is hypocrisy. Any of the virtues, if devoid of love, becomes worthless; for love is the basis of them all. The Pharisee refused to kiss Christ, and so the thermometer of love measured the falsehood of his intentions. He kissed all the other guests—an outward gesture for the sake of mere show—but failed to act when it came to God. His kisses to the others then were mere lies. The woman entered and gave the Pharisee neither kiss nor salute nor even respect; but when it came to the Lord, she prostrated her heart before Him. So this is our rule: love.

Holy Week

1980

Then indeed, even the first covenant had ordinances of divine service and the earthly sanctuary. For a tabernacle was prepared: the first part, in which was the lampstand, the table, and the showbread, which is called the sanctuary; and behind the second veil, the part of the tabernacle which is called the Holiest of All, which had the golden censer and the ark of the covenant overlaid on all sides with gold, in which were the golden pot that had the manna, Aaron's rod that budded, and the tablets of the covenant; and above it were the cherubim of glory overshadowing the mercy seat. Of these things we cannot now speak in detail.

Now when these things had been thus prepared, the priests always went into the first part of the tabernacle, performing the services. But into the second part the high priest went alone once a year, not without blood, which he offered for himself and for the people's sins committed in ignorance; the Holy Spirit indicating this, that the way into the Holiest of All was not yet made manifest while the first tabernacle was still standing.

"The Holy Spirit indicating this, that the way into the Holiest of All was not yet made manifest while the first tabernacle was still standing." Note that the passage is stating that, as long as the first tabernacle—that is, Solomon's Temple—still stood, the way into the Holy of Holies could not be revealed.

> *It was symbolic for the present time in which both gifts and sacrifices are offered which cannot make him who performed the service perfect in regard to the conscience—concerned only with foods and drinks, various washings, and fleshly ordinances imposed until the time of reformation.*
>
> *But Christ came as High Priest of the good things to come, with the greater and more perfect tabernacle not made with hands, that is, not of this creation.*

Pay close attention to these words: "the greater and more perfect tabernacle not made with hands." This phrase is repeated multiple times in the New Testament.

> *Not with the blood of goats and calves, but with His own blood He entered the Most Holy Place once for all, having obtained eternal redemption. For if the blood of bulls and goats and the ashes of a heifer, sprinkling the unclean, sanctifies for the purifying of the flesh, how much more shall the blood of Christ, who through the eternal Spirit offered Himself without spot to God, cleanse your conscience from dead works to serve the living God?[1]*

It's our habit to sit together every year at the opening of Holy Week, to review and understand the events about to happen; because during this week there is an abundance of biblical texts to be read, and an

---

1   Heb. 9:1–14

even greater abundance of rites to be performed. The man whose spirit is not alert will find himself preoccupied with the hymnology, the rituals, and the externals of the week, but will miss the heart and meaning of it all. This is one of the major sources of weakness among believers.

The Church from the very beginning laid its foundation by the Holy Spirit, and everything that was done and said within her was so through the Holy Spirit. If we neglect the Word and the relation of the Gospel to everything that is done within the Church, her rituals will become a lifeless heap. Our rituals are all based upon vital spiritual principles, and our hymns possess the most profound spiritual meanings; but if a person sits listlessly by, simply to listen to the pleasant music of the hymns and no more, contenting himself with an occasional remark such as, "My, what beautiful hymns I hear!"—such an attitude thrusts him utterly outside the pale of the Gospel. Once Holy Week is over, such a person is happy to reflect on how much he enjoyed praying Holy Week in such-and-such a church, where the rites were performed with the most fastidious attention to detail. This attitude does not inquire into the meaning of any rites or hymns, but is merely content with external particulars; and the Church thus grows weaker from year to year and from generation to generation.

And so, the Church has strayed from the source of her Light and from her great mission in the world. This terrifies me. As I have said many times before, whenever I sit with you or stand at the pulpit, my main objective is to communicate to the listener's mind the theological message of the hymns and rites performed during our feasts. The goal of my entire life is to clarify the spiritual meanings hidden in the traditions of the Church. But I will not hide from you the fact that this year, I considered not coming and speaking to you during Holy Week. I am quite tired, and ill, and have little strength to focus my attention on anything. I thought to give myself a break this year. So

I took to reading some books about Holy Week just for my personal edification; and I began with Palm Sunday, the great inaugural event of the week. I then encountered a verse spoken by Christ that bound all the incidents of Holy Week together and fused them into a consistent whole in my mind.

This verse is this: "Destroy this temple, and in three days I will raise it up."[2] It is a curious thing that He said this on Palm Sunday. On that day He entered the city as its King and not as its subject, a thing that infuriated the chief priests; and they demanded that He put a stop to the hosannas of the people. It was quite clear He was being recognized as the Messiah. He replied that, if they were to keep quiet, the stones would immediately cry out. In other words, He was confirming the people's hosannas: the Messiah was finally visiting His temple, as it was written of old. The implication was that the temple was *His*.

When He noticed the sheep, the oxen, the doves, and the money-changers, He made a flagellum of cords and drove the whole crowd clear out of the building. He told them that His Father's house was one of prayer but that they had made it a den of thieves. Then He makes the strange comment about destroying and rebuilding the temple. It seems almost unsuitable. Why cleanse the temple if you intend to destroy it afterwards? A person who expends so much effort in the cleansing would give the impression that he intends to begin a work of reformation and renovation of the temple.

But from the start, Christ plainly intended to initiate a clash with the temple rulers. The triumphal entry on the donkey, the acclamations of the disciples, the uproar of the city, the messianic hurrahs— all this was deeply disturbing to the chief priests. So they hurried forth and accosted Christ with the question, "By what authority are You doing these things? And what sign will You show us?" That is,

2   John 2:19

"We need a reason for Your boldness in claiming the kingship like this." When a sign was demanded of Him on a previous occasion, He told them, "An evil and adulterous generation seeks after a sign; and no sign will be given to it except the sign of the prophet Jonah"[3]—the theme of death and resurrection. When Christ says things like this, He is speaking to those who have ears to hear.

Solomon's temple was a wonder of wonders to the Jews. It was a place of utmost sanctity to them, since it was the sacred throne-room of God. He who swore by the temple swore by its Divine Inhabitant.[4] What audacity, then, did this Man have in suggesting the destruction of this holy place!

I want to provide a temporary solution to this problem until we find the complete solution at the end of our discussion. The Gospel remarks that "He was speaking of the temple of His body."[5] That is true, but Christ also intended His words to sentence the physical temple itself; because He says at another time that not one stone would remain upon another.[6] In this whole affair the collision between the Jewish rulers and Christ reaches its very zenith. The reaction of the chief priests—who were considered the guardians of the temple— was to resolve upon His death. He who threatened to destroy the holy building could not be left alive.

The Jews' understanding of Christ's words as pointing to the literal demolition of the temple comes out during His trial before Caiaphas: "Then some rose up and bore false witness against Him, saying, 'We heard Him say, "I will destroy this temple made with hands, and within three days I will build another made without hands."'"[7] It's obvious that the temple made *without* hands was that new human

---

3   Matt. 12:39
4   Matt. 23:21
5   John 2:21
6   Matt. 24:2
7   Mark 14:57

temple which was resurrected on the third day. The temple made *with* hands was that material building which the Jews said took forty-six years to build.[8] The point I'm trying to make is that the destruction of the temple our Lord talks about indicates, firstly, the death of His Body, and secondly, the demolition of Solomon's temple. This double meaning is important.

We want to understand what Christ meant by "destroy this temple," and why He directed the phrase at the chief priests. *Destroy this temple* is the thematic undercurrent running straight from Palm Sunday to Resurrection Sunday; it's the whole thrust of Holy Week. After Christ teaches for three years, He arrives at the final week to these conclusions: *Impossible* was the reconciliation of that nation with the truth; *impossible* was the reformation of their Law; and their temple *must* be destroyed. Nonetheless, it *would be raised up* in three days.

It is true that besides this, Christ offered a multitude of very rich teachings during those last days. But the overarching message He was declaring was the abolition of the old religion—not with stones and machinery, but by annulment of its legal primacy and authority. The true Temple of God, His Father's "House," could never be destroyed; what was to be destroyed was the fraud and deceit being offered to God under the guise of worship. What was aimed at was the distortions and dishonesty of the Rabbis and Pharisees—calculated to swell their pockets and make them the sole powers that could bind and loose souls. As Christ's reproof had it, they "bind heavy burdens, hard to bear, and lay them on men's shoulders, but they themselves will not move them with one of their fingers."[9] They perverted the knowledge of God and used it to serve themselves.

St. Paul's teaching is absolutely true: "The law is spiritual, but I

8 John 2:20
9 Matt. 23:4

am carnal, sold under sin."[10] For what was the essence of the Law? It was man's relationship to God. Had they but honestly and sincerely obeyed the precepts of the Law, it would have raised them to a higher sphere of living, and Christ's words would have come to them as the true Light. But they took the keys of knowledge and concealed them.[11] This is what Christ's rebukes were aimed at: the corruption of that religion which was supposed to bring man close to God.

Here we come to an important point. Why did Christ feel it such an urgent business to point out and rebuke the religious fraud before Him? It was because He was the Truth, and the fraud before Him had arrayed itself in the robes of truth. A stormy collision was inevitable. You see, sometimes our natural reasoning asks why Christ appeared so stern. "Were not His actions inconsistent with His usual kindness, and courtesy, and compassion?" "Was not His sharp toughness during Holy Week unlike the soft niceness we always attribute to Him?" Absolutely not. Christ is the Truth; and in the presence of deception, pretense, and fraud, the Truth can never be nice. Christ would act meekly toward sinners, but never toward those imposters of religion.

Why was He so aggressive in cleansing the temple? Think about it. Twenty percent of all the shekels paid to the temple went directly to the chief priests, and the regular priests and Levites made sure they got their share of the income as well. After any major feast, I imagine they would sit for at least three to four months arguing over the distribution of the money that came in. It was a detailed and elaborate system that needed a computer to keep track of everything. The whole ordeal really did result in a den of thieves.

Christ stood up to this enormous system of fraud in order to challenge it. *And He was intentionally launching Holy Week.* When He said

10   Rom. 7:14
11   Luke 11:52

"destroy this temple," He meant it. By that phrase He meant the end of the great organization of theft and deceit that existed, and He also meant the rise of their premeditated scheme to achieve His death. As their conspiracy began to crystallize, Christ began to raise His head high and to expand His chest, because this is what He wanted. This was His true Holy Week. "Shall I not drink the cup which My Father has given Me?"[12] He not only took the cup but even *mixed it* for the drinking!

If you read through Christ's trials during Holy Week, you will see that He never once offered an ounce of resistance to anyone: neither to Annas, nor Caiaphas, nor Herod, nor Pilate. "Are You not speaking to me? Do You not know that I have power to crucify You, and power to release You?"[13] But Christ says nothing in reply. Why? Did He desire to die just for dying's sake? No, He refused to respond to His accusers in order to silently expose the lies that lay hidden in their words. The ultimate exposure of their deception was His death on the Cross. They said, "It is expedient for us that one man should die for the people, and not that the whole nation should perish,"[14] and "If we let Him alone like this, everyone will believe in Him, and the Romans will come and take away both our place and nation."[15] Their minds were fixated only on their land, on their prestige, on their wealth, and on their position. Christ didn't utter just a general criticism of all the religious leaders, but persistently rebuked them on every particular lie and defect of which they were guilty.

Let me give you an illustration to clarify my meaning. Think of Saul of Tarsus as equivalent to the old temple. He was raised at the feet of Gamaliel, deeply immersed in the Law, and learned in the

---

12 John 18:11
13 John 19:10
14 John 11:50
15 John 11:48

precepts of the Old Testament—in other words, a main pillar in that old temple Christ sought to abolish. Saul was zealous for the Law and an enthusiast for rabbinical teaching, and these are what made him despise the name of Jesus. The end met by this Jesus was a proof that He was cursed, for "cursed is everyone who hangs on a tree."[16] And so His identity needed to be blotted out from Israel's rolls, because a crucified person was a shameful blot that rendered the nation unclean. A crucified person's corpse was buried far outside the gate of the city, and his name was erased from his tribe's family registry.

This is how Jesus of Nazareth appeared to Saul, and this is why he was so zealous in killing those who called upon that name. He dragged men, women, and children to prison—it mattered not—and utilized every means available to annihilate the Church. So as he was on his way to Damascus,[17] the greatness of that Law and the glory of those traditions that constituted his entire self-worth as a Pharisee were blown to bits by the realization that he was about to kill the Lord of Glory. It was his very frenzied obsession about the Law that was impelling him to persecute the Lord and blaspheme His name. And so, Paul's conversion was fierce and irreversible.

That is what the temple amounted to in Christ's mind. That is why He said it must be destroyed, and not one stone would remain upon another. The historical destruction of the temple itself was something of a miracle. The pyramids and temple at Karnak[18] both predate the Jerusalem temple by three thousand years, yet are still standing; and the Jewish temple's stones were no less massive than those of Karnak. But all the Israelis have left today is a tiny remnant of the old city wall

---

16 Gal. 3:13
17 Acts 9
18 The most famous surviving temple in Egypt, located in modern Luxor or ancient Thebes, impressive for the magnitude of its structures and the beauty of its ancient ornamentation.

still standing, which they've named the "wailing wall," because they go to lean against it and weep. If one stone from the original temple were ever found, they would immediately turn it into an object of worship. Yet not a single one is left! You see here the absolute fulfillment of God's decrees. Not one remnant, not one artifact, not one little piece of jewelry is left from that ancient temple!

Some archeologists have said that the modern Dome of the Rock[19] is built directly upon the location of the old temple; so the Jews used machines to burrow a tunnel beneath the Rock to see if they could find any trace of the temple. The Muslims of course rose up in protest because they feared the cavity being excavated below would cause the entire Dome of the Rock to collapse. And all this just to find a few stones! But it's no use. God had decreed it. "My house shall be called a house of prayer, but you have made it a 'den of thieves.'"[20]

This is the key to understanding how and why Holy Week began. The temple *had* to be destroyed, because "The Holy Spirit indicating this, that the way into the Holiest of All was not yet made manifest *while the first tabernacle was still standing.*" The idea that the way into the Holiest could not be revealed while the first temple stood was buried deep in Christ's heart; and it's the reason He strove so earnestly (though sorrowfully) to put an end to the first temple.

But of course, He wouldn't do it like certain people today, who say to each other, "Hey, there's a Christian church, let's destroy it," and use fire and weaponry to attack it. That's a superficial thing, really. What is *inside* the church can never be destroyed. They might see red brick from the outside, but it is made of living stones on the inside; they see a foundation of stone beneath, but its true roots are from on high.

---

19   Famous Islamic shrine situated at the visual center of Jerusalem's Temple Mount, the very place believed to be the location of the ancient Jewish temple. It has taken the place of the Jewish temple as the Holy City's most recognizable landmark.

20   Matt. 21:13

The Church is a single Body, against which all the powers of earth, and government, and Satan's legions, and hell itself cannot prevail. And why? Because Christ is risen. This is a Body which has died and risen again from death! It cannot be killed again. Just as there are non-flammable fabrics produced today, so is the Church "non-flammable." It is "non-destroyable." If her Head is up in heaven, then will her enemies ever find a ladder high enough to attack it? If her stones are living, then they cannot be destroyed by machines. The mortar that seals the stones together is the Holy Spirit; He binds us heart to heart, soul to soul, heaven to earth. Never make the mistake of thinking that the Church of Christ is built with human hands.

✠ ✠ ✠

Until this day, temples are being erected all around the world in the name of false religions and false worship, for the sake of halting the worship of Christ Jesus. The world today is reeling from division and conflict because it has rejected the mystery of the Incarnation. The world lived in darkness until the day came for the Son of God to give it the spirit of sonship. Man was supposed to become a son of God, and all men to be brothers of each other. But it was all supposed to be founded upon the Incarnation. We need to receive this spirit of sonship, not in theory, but in reality.

The world lacks this spirit, and the world lacks brotherhood, and this is its great dilemma. A person who does not live in sonship to God cannot live in proper sonship even to his own father. Rather, that relationship would mimic the relationship of, say, a cat to its father. That is, while still young it trails behind its father licking his feet; and when it grows old, it bites and scratches, then abandons him. This is the type of "sonship" that predominates on earth.

It need not be so with humanity! The day Christ was made known on earth, humanity was raised up, family was raised up, social life was raised up, and the different sectors of society were brought together by the highest and greatest bonds that could ever exist between human beings. Even hospitals were brought into existence as a result of Christ's appearance. For a hospital is a place of *hospitality*. It has taken its name from a word indicating the act of receiving another human being with the best and tenderest of manners possible.

Again, that bond of sonship should have brought us all together in Christ and advanced us to God as blameless children. When a boy goes to his father and says, "Daddy, I want this and that," if the father asks, "Why do you seem so sure that I will give it to you?" the boy will respond, "Because you love me." This is verbatim how the Bible describes our relationship with God: "We have confidence and access to the Father through faith in Christ."[21] We've lost this confidence. We're still living in that old temple that needs to be abolished.

Destroy this temple—how I pray and beseech the Lord Jesus that He would renew that call! Oh, that He would destroy this false temple in which one man makes an enemy out of his human brother in the name of God! Did the chief priests kill Christ in order to do honor to God? Did the priests and elders really find it such a good idea to murder the Messiah? Did humanity really approach this most perilous edge of falsehood?

Yet if Christ had not died, there would have been no Resurrection, and the re-creation of man would not have happened. The destruction of the temple thus indicates the transition from all things old to new. The difference between *old* and *new* is as significant as the difference between Solomon's temple and Christ Himself. The death and Resurrection of our Lord made possible the transition from man in his old state to man in his new state. What is the old man, and what is the new man? The old man lived in the old temple; and since Christ

---

21   Paraphrase of Eph. 3:12.

took His body from the Virgin Mary—according to our tradition, while she was still living in the temple as a young girl—He took the Body directly from that temple. Thus the phrase *destroy this temple* points to the destruction of humanity's old temple and the construction of humanity's new temple—which man will "put on" just as he originally put on the body of dust. "As we have borne the image of the man of dust, we shall also bear the image of the heavenly Man."[22]

Finally, just as the old man worshiped in Solomon's temple, so the new man worships in Christ Jesus. What does it mean to worship in Christ Jesus? It's a liturgical concept, because living "in" Christ points to baptism, and Eucharist, and Scripture-reading, and biblical asceticism, and daily spiritual struggle. *Life in Christ* thus also equates with *life in the Church.* Christ is in His Church, and He leads us on "to the unity of the faith and of the knowledge of the Son of God, to a perfect man, to the measure of the stature of the fullness of Christ."[23]

To sum up, this is the key to understanding Holy Week: It heralds the imminent end of a sham worship, which failed to nourish the spiritual needs of humanity, and the establishment of a true worship offered in spirit and in truth—not dependent upon material stones, but upon Christ, who is the foundation and liturgy of the New Temple.

---

22 1 Cor. 15:49
23 Eph. 4:13

Feast of the Ascension

1979

We now reach the final step in our Lord's plan of salvation, and our beautiful Church traditions help us to enter deeply into His life. Just the other day we were walking with Christ through His sufferings; then suddenly the Resurrection came, and the Church raised its voice in rejoicing. We were given the privilege to proclaim a new life for man, how the doors of our tombs were flung open and we emerged alive. If we lived as deeply in our faith as the Spirit would wish us to, I tell you we would never be satisfied enough with the blessings of Pascha to move on to the Resurrection feast; and we would never be satisfied enough with the Resurrection to move on to the Ascension. But man is quick to forget; and the Spirit uses this weakness of ours to our advantage, in moving us along from feast to feast—or, as it were, from mountain peak to mountain peak, that we might catch glimpses of that heavenly sunlight as we travel toward eternity.

I found it very difficult myself to enter into contemplation about the Ascension because of the power of the Resurrection that had dominated my soul. I was consoled with the strength of the Resurrection that lifts me above the dust and soil of this world—and now, for Christ to be taken out of my sight is a hard thing! But we can receive consolation from the Ascension if we only experience its power.

Every stage in Christ's redemptive work had to it a peculiar power. But the important point is to move from the mere *news* of an event to its actual *life*. The Nativity as news, for example, is a pleasant story. We tell it to the kids and build little manger scenes and perform plays and have a jolly time. But what then? We have our parties and give out sweets and celebrate Santa Claus, and that's the end of it. The living power of Christmas remains absent: it's just *news*. This is what grieves Christ and His Church, that we live only on the *news* of redemption. But we should be experiencing the actual power of Christmas entering our lives, and feeling Christmas to be a real gift brought down from heaven; and similarly regarding the rest of the Lord's life. As mere story, the Gospel events are interesting to the hearer only to the extent that the speaker is talented in storytelling. But the living experience of a redemptive event provides the believer with lasting satisfaction.

Each of our Lord's divine acts begins at a certain point in time but nevertheless has its origin before time began. They begin in the eternal past and endure into the eternal future; therefore, when you enter deeply into His work, you seize both ends of eternity at once. Doesn't St. John say, "In the beginning was the Word," indicating a beginning *before* time? (In contrast, when Genesis says, "In the beginning God created the heavens and the earth," it is indicating a beginning *in* time.)

When a man lives deeply in these transcendent truths, they nourish and satisfy his soul and cause him to live beyond the normal bounds of his existence. He becomes aware of an Existence above all other existent things—beyond the sun, the moon, the earth; beyond life and death itself. This is the apex of spirituality: that a person enter a state of being beyond his mere temporal life. Temporal existence never brings *joy*; it can provide only leisure or entertainment. But when a person takes up a transcendent and eternal existence, it is like returning to the paradise of Eden.

I invite you all to claim this right you have in Christ Jesus. It brings an indescribable peace to the soul. If you live solely on the news of redemption, you will grow tired of the Bible and of religious books. But once you enter into its divine truth, your mind will begin to wander into the realms of heaven as "deep calls unto deep," and the religious book will unconsciously slip out of your hands as the spiritual reverie absorbs your thoughts. At that point the whole range of your questions, your doubts, and your mental perplexities will fall away of themselves. They lose their negative potency, not because they receive answers, but because their every answer is Christ. Christ Himself responds to your every objection and dismisses it. You finally find yourself free of those perplexing questions which you were unable to resolve, and which themselves can only produce a state of mental illness.

You see, if you have an acute craving for something but are denied it, you become ill. Say a man has an intense desire to see the Virgin Mary. He begins to pray to the Virgin and the angels about his desire, but his spiritual and theological maturity are not equal to it. In time he may become delusional and think the Virgin appears to him on a regular basis, and he carries on conversation with her and the saints. His mind develops a sort of schizophrenia; he requires psychiatric treatment.

There is a story from the early desert fathers in which a monk suddenly announces to the rest, "Hello everyone, I am now a bishop." "How?" they ask. He replies, "The Virgin Mary came to me in the middle of the night and ordained me." "You need our help," they cried.

They seized him, locked him in a cell, and fed him a diet of water and coarse bread until he snapped out of his delusion. Man is ever prone to fall away from the truth and to deviate from his proper aim, which is Christ.

✝ ✝ ✝

Let's now talk about the Ascension. Christ said, "I tell you the truth. It is to your advantage that I go away; for if I do not go away, the Helper will not come to you; but if I depart, I will send Him to you."[1] The Holy Spirit would come and clarify to their minds all the previous events that had occurred.

There are several different expressions in the New Testament that point to the Ascension. For example, "The Son of Man must be lifted up, that whoever believes in Him should not perish but have eternal life."[2] This *lifted up* indicates at once the Cross, the Resurrection, and the Ascension together. He also said, "And I, if I am lifted up from the earth, will draw all peoples to Myself."[3] Again, He says to Mary Magdalene, "Go to My brethren and say to them, 'I am ascending to My Father and your Father, and *to* My God and your God.'"[4]

When we thus reflect on the Lord's foretelling of these events, and then their happy accomplishment, we feel the Gospel crystallizing or coming to be as we read. For the essence of the Gospel, the *evangelion*, is joy. (*Ev-* indicates something good, beautiful, or joyful; and *angelio* indicates something told or proclaimed.) Today we see the same accomplishment: We read how Christ charged Mary Magdalene with the message to the disciples that He would be ascending soon; and after forty days, He ascends.

---

1   John 16:7
2   John 3:14
3   John 12:32
4   John 20:17

So what is the Ascension all about? In 1975, we spoke at length on this topic, but mostly from a biblical and theological point of view. Today I would like to add to that discussion an additional spiritual and consolatory dimension that was perhaps lacking.

We had said that the Ascension of the Lord in a cloud and His sitting at the right hand of the Majesty was a sign of His entrance into the heavenly Holy of Holies and His receiving all authority from the Father. Now, Daniel the Prophet prophesied about this event—though without realizing its significance—as he sat by the rivers of Babylon in exile. And note, God's most beautiful visions are always sent to man during times of trial. Men living in comfort and ease cannot receive consolatory visions from God. But when a person suffers outward stresses and inward strains, and in his anxiety seeks the face of God with tears, he straightway obtains divine succor. "Your comforts delight my soul."[5]

Daniel says,

> I was watching in the night visions,
> And behold, One like the Son of Man,
> Coming with the clouds of heaven!
> He came to the Ancient of Days,
> And they brought Him near before Him.
> Then to Him was given dominion and glory and a kingdom,
> That all peoples, nations, and languages should serve Him.
> His dominion is an everlasting dominion.[6]

In the Old Testament, cloud and smoke were usually associated with the Divine Presence, as when (for example) a dark and stormy cloud

---

5   Ps. 94:19
6   Dan. 7:13, 14

engulfed Mount Sinai.[7] In speaking of "clouds," therefore, Daniel knows exactly what he's talking about. He says, "The visions of my head troubled me." Why, O Daniel? Aren't these prophetic words easy to comprehend? But no! Who is this Son of Man? Who is this that approaches the Ancient of Days to receive a kingdom? A person who is given dominion over the kingdom of God should be worshiped! But lo, I am an Israelite, and there is only one God, and He alone is worthy of worship! "Hear, O Israel: The LORD our God, the LORD *is* one!"[8] So what is this prophecy about, O Lord? An unknown Son of Man approaches an indescribable Ancient of Days to receive domin- ion, "that all peoples, nations, and languages should serve Him"—but this is the status of Yahweh Himself!

Daniel is speaking here about the Ascension: "He ascended into heaven and sat at the right hand of the Father."[9] We also have the testimony of St. Paul: "Therefore God also has highly exalted Him and given Him the name which is above every name;"[10] and again, "He is far above all principality and power and might and dominion, and every name that is named, not only in this age but also in that which is to come;"[11] and in Hebrews, I believe, he writes, "For such a High Priest was fitting for us, who is holy, harmless, undefiled, sep- arate from sinners, and has become higher than the heavens."[12] He lived just like us, that is, eating and drinking and all, until they put Him on a cross like a common man, buried Him in a tomb like a common man—and He emerged from the tomb and ascended into heaven, like no other man. It was essential that He be utterly unique among humanity, totally "separate from sinners," and this was realized

---

7   Ex. 19:16
8   Deut. 6:4
9   Nicene Creed
10   Phil. 2:9
11   Eph. 1:21
12   Heb. 7:26

at the Ascension. These meditations are just light brushes on the theology of it.

But what is *our* role in it? It is this: "God raised us up together, and made us sit together in the heavenly places in Christ Jesus."[13] That is to say, Christ did not ascend alone; He ascended *bearing our humanity*: we ascended with Him! As it's stated in the theology of St. Paul, we are the members of His body, His very flesh and bones.[14] He is the head of the Church, and we are its members.[15]

There is another image in Scripture of profound depth that may benefit us here. Christ once told the disciples, "I am the true vine, and you are the branches."[16] I used to think this image intended to envisage us as the branches being attached to Him as the vine or trunk of the plant. I hadn't noticed one thing: The vine and the branches are the same thing. When Christ said, "I am the vine," He was including the branches as well. This very subtle and mystical meaning had always eluded me! In its deep and mystical impenetrability, it is a concept no less esoteric than that of the Holy Trinity in one God. Here is a mystery you cannot mentally grasp; I can only continue to speak about it until it *touches* you. You cannot understand it, but you can feel it. "I am the vine, and you are the branches."

Imagine removing the branches completely from the plant: what would be left of the vine? Anything? Thus, when Christ says, "I am the vine," He means to say that He is the whole thing. Ah, how wonderful! This conception is loftier even than St. Paul's image of Christ as the head and us as the body; for Paul's image is *partitional*, that is, he analyzes the relationship into its separate parts—head and body— in order to make it easy for the understanding. Anyone can imagine himself as a member in the body controlled and guided by the Head.

---

13 Eph. 2:6
14 1 Cor. 12
15 Col. 1:18
16 John 15:5

But the image Christ uses is *holistic,* that is, it joins us and Himself into a simple, single entity. The analogy of the vine renders any separation between us and Him impossible.

And this conception leads us on to further thoughts. He says, "Every branch in Me that does not bear fruit He takes away; and every branch that bears fruit He prunes, that it may bear more fruit."[17] The fruitless branch is not cast out simply because it is unproductive, and the fruitful branch is not tended and pruned just because it is helpful. What I mean is that a branch is not kept or severed for its own sake, but rather for the sake of the vine. In other words, Christ handles the branches for the sake of His own health, because the fruit that grows does not ultimately belong to the branches but to the vine. Can a vine thrive without fruit? Can a dry and barren vine subsist? So when Christ chooses which branches to preserve, His concern is His very sustenance.

Another verse says, "We are God's handiwork."[18] Could God ever abide without producing work? Physically, yes; He is not in need of this entire creation. But spiritually, no: God cannot exist without spiritual work—*God is love.* So we produce fruit because Christ has given us Himself, and taken us up into Himself, and united us with Himself. We are now a part of the "I" that constitutes His Self. Therefore, so long as you are infatuated with your own "I," with your own identity, He cannot work through you. But if you are a *branch,* attached to the trunk and inseparable from the other branches, then you are a genuine part of the vine. And thence you will say, "It is not I who live, but Christ lives in me."[19] The "I" that you write in quotation marks to indicate your own personal identity will no longer be yours, but Christ's.

---

17 John 15:2
18 Eph. 2:10
19 Gal. 2:20

With these thoughts in mind, let us include a few more words on Christ's Ascension. He did not ascend because of any inherent necessity, or as though He were earthly and needed to go up to be heavenly. We have agreed that He is in the Father and one essence with the Father and can never be separated from the paternal bosom. Therefore, He ascended *for us* and *with us*. The point of this feast is that it is *our Ascension*. If Christ hadn't ascended, it would have been absolutely impossible for any man walking this earth to be saved. The Ascension tears down all limits, too; in Christ, we may boldly approach the Father. In Hebrews we read, "Therefore, brethren, having boldness to enter the Holiest by the blood of Jesus, by a new and living way which He consecrated for us, through the veil, that is, His flesh."[20] So this upward ascent to the Father is our own, and the road to Him that was once blocked is now made open.

The honest truth is, brethren, that the Ascension returned to Adam the original honor that was once his. Today, the second Adam has opened the door to paradise and restored to humanity its original dignity. He has allowed man not just to live with Him, but to sit enthroned with Him. Man no longer needs to hide under a tree; he can never again be expelled from paradise. The Bridegroom has taken us into His chamber and shut the door.[21] I take great pleasure in the notion that the door will be shut. Of course, we do not want to be shut out like the five foolish virgins. But if we are counted among the wise, and Christ draws us in and closes the door, I will ask Him to lock it securely. Why? So we can't walk out again the way Adam did!

It is finished: He entered the most holy place to achieve for us eternal redemption.[22] When He entered the most holy place, He entered carrying our own nature: that is, carrying *you*. He entered carrying

---

20   Heb. 10:19, 20
21   Matt. 25:10
22   Heb. 9:24

your weak, wavering nature. Or perhaps I should say He entered bearing your *name* (to avoid the quibble theologians are apt to raise when they hear talk of the meeting between human and divine natures). Remember that He did not enter bearing His august name, "The Living Son of God," but bearing your lowly individual name.

Again, this is *our* Ascension, and the sitting at the right hand of the Father is *ours*—because Christ is not situated to the Father's right, for He is *in* the Father and the Father *in* Him. The older theologians were often confused when commenting on this doctrine. They said that the sitting at the right hand shows Christ's equality and co-eternality with the Father, forgetting the Son's complete unity with the Father in essence. Christ's sitting at His right hand is solely by virtue of the fact that He ascended with the flesh of mankind. Man's flesh has no place in the eternal essence of the Father, but it is honored instead with the right-hand position next to Him. Tell me, who sits to the right of a human father at suppertime? The eldest son. (Our own table is modeled on this pattern.) So in the person of Christ we have the glory of nearness to the Holy Trinity! It is all through Christ, and without Him, we are strangers outside the gate.

I want to linger a little longer on the idea of the kingdom. "To Him was given dominion and glory and a kingdom."[23] On this point, too, the theologians and commentators tend to suffer from shortsightedness, as frankly you and I do as well. Fortunately, though, the illuminating seasons and feasts of the Church refocus our vision and correct the errors in our thinking.

I used to think Christ was to take the kingdom and its authority for Himself. But He does not want it. "I did not come to judge the world."[24] He did not come, that is, to be a judge and ruler over the world. He came to save it. But in the scheme of things, the Father

---

23 Dan. 7:14
24 John 12:47

had to give all authority into the hands of the Son to accomplish the world's salvation. "Who is it who judges but He who justifies?"[25] Well, if He who sits to judge me is also the one who intends to acquit me, then my innocence is secured. We see then, Abbas, that Christ did not receive the kingly authority for His own good, but for our justification. Did you think He wanted merely to *rule*? Rule over what? Did you suppose He desired to be monarch over you or the archangels or the cherubim? He desires none of it. He took the kingdom in order to hand it over to us.

These are astounding words, so listen closely.

> *I was watching in the night visions,*
> *And behold, One like the Son of Man,*
> *Coming with the clouds of heaven!*
> *He came to the Ancient of Days,*
> *And they brought Him near before Him.*
> *Then to Him was given dominion and glory and a kingdom.*[26]

So where are we in this picture? Well, did you notice the title *Son of Man*? Is it obvious enough? Maybe it isn't. Then let's further consider the passage:

> *I, Daniel, was grieved in my spirit within my body, and the visions*
> *of my head troubled me. I came near to one of those who stood by,*
> *and asked him the truth of all this. So he told me and made known*
> *to me the interpretation of these things. "Those great beasts, which*
> *are four, are four kings which arise out of the earth."*[27]

---

25 See Rom. 8:33.
26 Dan. 7:13, 14
27 Dan. 7:15, 16

The beasts are atrocious figures to which I will return presently. "But the saints of the Most High shall receive the kingdom, and possess the kingdom forever, even forever and ever." Ah, from whom will they receive it? From Him to whom it was given! I think Christ will appear so beautifully majestic in this picture that you won't be able to endure it. The usual image we have of the Reigning Christ is of one who sits luxuriantly on a throne like a great chief, or a Pantocrator, with little saints prostrating at His feet. But it's not correct. He took the kingdom *in order to give it to us.* There is even more to be said on this point: "'But the court shall be seated, and they shall take away his dominion, to consume and destroy *it* forever."[28] This refers to the beasts and kings and troublesome enemies who will all come to nothing.

> *Then the kingdom and dominion,*
> *And the greatness of the kingdoms under the whole heaven,*
> *Shall be given to the people, the saints of the Most High.*
> *His kingdom is an everlasting kingdom,*
> *And all dominions shall serve and obey Him.*[29]

We are the "everlasting kingdom," for we will reign eternally with Him! This is the end of the matter as described by Daniel. Now, when we go back to Revelation, we read that the saints will reign with Him for a thousand years.[30]   And Christ Himself says,

> *"But you are those who have continued with Me in My trials. And I bestow upon you a kingdom, just as My Father bestowed one upon Me, that you may eat and drink at My table in My kingdom, and sit on thrones judging the twelve tribes of Israel."*[31]

---

28   Dan. 7:26
29   Dan. 7:27
30   Rev. 20:6
31   Luke 22:28

See, He is telling the disciples they will one day judge. St. Paul further says, "Do you not know that the saints will judge the world? . . . Do you not know that we shall judge angels?"[32] Ah, when you gather all these Old and New Testament statements together, what a glorious inheritance you realize we have! The words of prophets, patriarchs, and Christ Himself all merge to point toward the Ascension. And this to the end that we might reign with Him—not just that we might avoid death, or escape the judgment, but that we might *judge*. We once lay under the judgment of death (by the Law); but when Christ ascended, He pulled us out from under that burden and lifted us up to be the very possessors of the judgment.

☩ ☩ ☩

By the Cross, we received the blood of Christ. By the Resurrection, we were born again to new life. By the Ascension, we were given the Kingdom. Daniel (as we said) alluded to it. Christ alluded to it in His eucharistic discourse[33] and clearly told them before His sufferings that they would be enthroned with Him in the Kingdom. The Revelation alludes to it by saying that Christ "has made us kings and priests to His God and Father."[34]

Where were all these scriptural quotations before? Were they too scattered to come to our notice? But today they are converging like rays of light to reveal an essential truth. I don't even know how they all turned up today, since I hadn't written them down or prepared them in advance. But these rays of light have served to brighten this glorious day!

As I said, I had approached this day with some trepidation,

---

32 1 Cor. 6:2, 3
33 John 6:51
34 Rev. 1:6

because I had to leave behind the Resurrection with its unspeakable joys and glories. During those days I felt as if I were traversing the whole extent of Galilee, skirting Tiberias[35] over and over, pursuing the Resurrected Christ, enjoying the company of the disciples, straining my eyes to behold the Risen Lord, to hear His words and to touch His wounds. Then in the midst of this happy time, the Church suddenly tells me to stop: "Child, the forty days have come to an end." "But leave me here a little while longer!" "My son, listen to me. I am the Church, your Mother; with every season, I nurse you with new milk for the sake of your continued growth. You finished the Resurrection feeding, which made you shiny and plump. Now, it's time for the Ascension feeding."

A few questions to ponder: In what circumstances did these visions come to Daniel? And in what circumstances did Christ ascend to heaven? And in what circumstances did St. Paul and St. John write about the Ascension? Daniel's visions came during the Babylonian Captivity. Those were troubling times. How could an Israelite be exiled in Babylon? He was one of the chosen people; his were the covenant and the promises; his was the true God. How could he then be forsaken in a foreign captivity? These sentiments of estrangement are captured in the exilic psalm[36] whose depth of feeling can make stones weep:

> By the rivers of Babylon,
> There we sat down, yea, we wept
> When we remembered Zion.
> We hung our harps
> Upon the willows in the midst of it.[37]

---

35 I.e., the Sea of Galilee
36 Ps. 137
37 Ps. 137:1, 2

Do you know what these willows are? This is a type of tree that sprouts profusely by the Nile, which you will have seen if you ever rode the train in that direction. You find this tree bending over toward the river, dropping down its branches into the water, and the dangling branches somewhat resemble a girl's hair, which is another name the tree takes in Arabic. I'm planning to plant one of these in the monastery that you might never forget it. It's a tree that *weeps*. The psalm chose the perfect tree for its image. How marvelous was the poetic spirit of Jewish psalmody! The Israelites hung their harps upon its branches in mourning over their plight, while their captors came and requested to hear one of their famous songs of mirth. They responded with an adamant refusal:

> *How shall we sing the Lord's song*
> *In a foreign land?*
> *If I forget you, O Jerusalem,*
> *Let my right hand forget its skill!*
> *If I do not remember you,*
> *Let my tongue cling to the roof of my mouth—*
> *If I do not exalt Jerusalem*
> *Above my chief joy.*[38]

In this atmosphere, the news came to Daniel that he would be thrown into the den of lions. He then lay down to sleep and saw a terrifying dream of four beasts with hideous features doing this and that, and he was in utter shock. In midst of this turmoil he says, "I was watching in the night visions, and behold, One like the Son of Man." The superficial reader will not see the significance of the appearance of the Son of Man at this point.

Continuing the vision in the next chapter, he speaks of a goat,

---

38 Ps. 137:4–6

saying, "And out of one of them came a little horn which grew exceedingly great toward the south, toward the east, and toward the Glorious Land. And it grew up to the host of heaven; and it cast down *some* of the host and *some* of the stars to the ground, and trampled them." Shocking! He throws about the stars as if they were rocks! "He even exalted himself as high as the Prince of the host"—that is, Christ—"and by him the daily *sacrifices* were taken away, and the place of His sanctuary was cast down." The removal of the sacrifices and the demolition of the sanctuary occurred during the Babylonian Exile. These were things that caused the Israelites' hearts to burn. "Because of transgression, an army was given over *to* the horn to oppose the daily sacrifices; and he cast truth down to the ground. He did all this and prospered."[39] My God, how could Daniel tolerate such a vision? That the evil one rise and cast truth down to the ground? And *succeed!* Where is God in all this? But here is Daniel's solution to the vile acts of the wicked one:

> *I was watching in the night visions,*
> *And behold, One like the Son of Man,*
> *Coming with the clouds of heaven!*
> *He came to the Ancient of Days,*
> *And they brought Him near before Him.*
> *Then to Him was given dominion and glory and a*
>   *kingdom.*[40]

There is, then, a hope of salvation, for man has a Son who will approach the Ancient of Days and will be given an everlasting kingdom. Remember that this vision came at a most dark time. Daniel was in exile, and he has just come out of the lions' den, and his head

---

39 Dan. 8:9–12
40 Dan. 7:13, 14

was now whirling. It was the same with St. Paul. He spoke about the Ascension and our future reign with Christ and so forth, but see what his life looked like! He would escape one disaster to enter into another; he was stoned, flogged, shipwrecked—a life of constant tension and bitterness. Then in the midst of it Christ appears to comfort him, and tells him that He will send him to the ends of the earth.[41]

It is man's recompense—a period of rest to counteract a period of pain. The Ascension into the Majesty, or the inauguration of the eternal kingdom, is the period of consolation and encouragement to counteract the bitter period of our current life. Even Christ ascended while Jerusalem was seething with unrest and the disciples were still being plotted against. The Resurrection did not cancel the hard realities of life. The Ascension did not protect the disciples from being arrested and beaten by their persecutors. And the author of the Revelation—who wrote that we would be "kings and priests" to the living God—was incarcerated on the island of Patmos. Patmos was nothing but a barren rock, studded with caves much deeper than the ones we inhabited in *el-Rayyan*;[42] and John was chained to the wall while his guard was outside tanning. And in this state he wrote that we would be kings and priests!

You see, the Ascension is the certificate of guarantee we've been given to frame and hang up in the face of our adversary who accuses us day and night. To the extent to which the affairs of life grow cruel against us, and to the extent to which the Church and Her people are besieged and threatened by enemies, to that extent and more is our faith in Christ strengthened, and so much more does the glorious Ascension become a light to our way, the certainty of our power, and the certainty of our inheritance in the everlasting Kingdom.

---

41 Acts 23:11

42 A remote and inhospitable locality in the Egyptian desert where Abba Matta and his followers passed approximately ten years of their lives, immediately prior to moving to the Monastery of St. Macarius.

The Holy Spirit and Pentecost

1979

Blessed be God, who has given us the privilege to hold a feast for the Holy Spirit. We have enjoyed sharing meditations on the various stages of our salvation, beginning with Holy Week, and culminating in our discussion on the Feast of the Ascension,[1] where we celebrated man's sitting at the right hand of Majesty—the greatest leap forward humanity has taken since the creation in Genesis.

Now think with me, beloved, on how much toil humanity has spent throughout its history, by its great literatures and philosophies, in its search for the truth and for the best way to articulate the truth. The majority of our thinkers and philosophers have held the opinion (and a mere deadweight intellectual opinion it is) that man has failed to fulfill the purpose of his existence. Many such thinkers have consequently lived in a state of melancholy. Many of them also entered into a state of apostasy and animosity toward God. The chief among them was the famous philosopher Nietzsche, who uttered profanities

---

1   See chapter 11.

against our belief in salvation, and whose motto ("God is dead") has been parroted by thinkers until this day. This idea was the sum of all his philosophizing: that since humanity is without a God, it must strive to fulfill its destiny on its own. This dark idea took hold of a large portion of humanity and cast it headlong into a pit. Later on there came the painful attempts to validate or verify the meaning of man's existence, which took on the name of existentialism. They could not see on the face of humanity, nor even on the face of the Church, anything encouraging about humanity's existence.

Man is weary; he seems to be forever running after truth and searching after peace, but in vain. He knows not where to find them. And not one epoch of humanity has been spared the ravages of division, terror, and war. This is the only picture of the world philosophy has beheld. The great literary authors consequently adopted this grim point of view and expressed it through their stories and poetry; and when you read them, they seem to ring everywhere with the sound of despair and betray the fact that their minds have given up all hope.

The one "hope" they might preserve is the idea that the growth of human knowledge will lead to progress in society, which will lead us on to a new age of enlightenment. But of course, that hasn't happened. Man is progressing before our eyes, but every age turns out as bad as the previous one. Neither knowledge, nor literature, nor philosophy, nor art, nor politics has been able to move humanity forward even by an inch. The Church herself has likewise failed to bequeath to the world a sound vision for the destiny of humankind. She is the guardian of an extremely precious mystery; but since the mystery has proven greater than her capability to express it, and greater than her courage to preach it, she has kept it to herself. The secret she conceals is the fact that man has been transposed from a dead decaying nature to a new and divine one.

We may have achieved a measure of our own natural progress;

we've created an elaborate array of philosophy and knowledge; our sculptures and painting and music are impressive; we've devised a very fine style of manners and society; we've made it possible for humans to enjoy a life of leisure and ease; even the orphans, disabled, and under-privileged have been made a focus of concern. But despite all this, man remains man. He has not become anything more. Not only so, but from the perspective of my age, looking back upon two whole gener-ations, I say that man is getting smaller, not bigger. His goodness, his humanity, his faith, his love, his trust, and his friendship are all quickly dwindling. Children are not what they were, parents are not what they were, and—forgive me for saying this—monks are not what they were. When you read about the first era of monasticism, you get a sense of the spiritual freedom, the humanness, the originality, and the courage of those hermits. These traits have shriveled up today.

Considering all this, it seems quite a leap to say that humanity has been raised from its lower mortal nature to the higher nature of the Resurrection. We live in the newness of spiritual life. Our names are written in heaven, not on earth. This was the thrust of theological discourse in the Orthodox Church during the first five centuries of the Christian era: God became man that men might becomes gods.[2] Christ told the disciples, "Tarry in the city of Jerusalem until you are endued with power from on high,"[3] which was the gift of the Holy Spirit. When you thus join the Incarnation to Pentecost in your mind, you come to the following result: Christ wore human nature, and we wore the Spirit. What an astounding leap for humanity!

But in vain do our scholars and thinkers try to achieve any other betterment for mankind. Man's ailments are the result of his being *man* and of nothing else. He's confined by his own nature. However, there has now been imported into his nature the ability to grow and

---

2   St. Athanasius
3   Luke 24:49

live with God. This mystery is hidden from the world and from its wise men, and all they can produce is jumbled and incoherent ideas. But let us not be incoherent too. We ought to know the truth about our origins and our destinies.

The work of the Holy Spirit is the culmination and seal of the entire plan of salvation. You know that on the special church occasions of every year, I have new meditations to share with you, and I never go back to the old books or articles I have written. I recently wondered to myself: When Pentecost was occurring at Jerusalem, what was happening here in the Egyptian desert? It was undoubtedly very still and quiet, but the Holy Spirit must have been hovering over the desert as He hovered over the waters of the void in Genesis.[4] So can it really be that the Spirit on Pentecost confined His movement strictly to that little area in Jerusalem? No; I feel sure that He came here as well, and my heart thrills to the thought that the Spirit—who came for the world's salvation—visited in fact many places all over the earth, in order that Christ might one day be glorified throughout all its lands.

How many hundreds of thousands of saints lived and died here in Egypt? How many lived here in the power of the Holy Spirit? Let us then review a few points regarding the Holy Spirit, that we might live this time together in His presence, and that we might grow, for tomorrow begins the season of the Holy Spirit.[5] During this time we ought to read everything we can about the Holy Spirit; and each one of us ought to have a close and real relationship with Him—one as close and real as our relationship with Christ and the Father.

---

4   Gen. 1:3

5   In the Coptic Church, the feast of Pentecost inaugurates the Apostles' Fast, which varies in length each year according to the date of Easter, and which is a celebration of the work of the Holy Spirit in the Church through the acts of the Apostles. It concludes with the Apostles' Feast.

✣ ✣ ✣

In the Old Testament, the work of the Holy Spirit involved using the prophets as mouthpieces to point toward Christ. The clearest expression of this comes from St. Peter's epistle, where we have a wonderfully concise description of the Spirit's work: "Of this salvation the prophets have inquired and searched carefully, who prophesied of the grace that would come to you, searching what, or what manner of time, the Spirit of Christ who was in them was indicating."[6] The prophets did indeed toil ceaselessly in contemplating the nature of the salvation that would come to future generations; and in the New Testament, the Spirit revealed that salvation by revealing Christ, and accorded to us His *grace*.

In every stage of salvation Christ passed through, He accomplished it *with* (and not just *by*) the Holy Spirit. Pay close attention, because I am using very precise theological terms here, and we don't want to err in this area. The second and third Hypostases[7] of the Trinity were working in unison from the first step of redemption. Christ was conceived in the womb of the Virgin *by the Holy Spirit*. At His Baptism in the Jordan, *the Spirit alighted upon Him*. When He worked miracles among the people and some charged Him with performing the works by Beelzebub, He told them they thus refused salvation by *resisting*

6 1 Pet. 1:10

7 "Hypostasis" (Gr. ὑπόστασις) in the Orthodox Church is equivalent to the *Prosopon* (Eng. "Person") of the Western churches, and it indicates the foundational being or substantive reality of a thing. The word is viewed as emphasizing the shared "substance" or "nature" (οὐσία) of the Holy Trinity, whereas "Person" may be misconstrued as indicating three disparate entities or beings. Historically speaking, because the Orthodox Church grew out of the soil of the East, it naturally inclined toward Greek terminology, while the Roman Church, being a growth of the West, bears a natural affinity toward Latin.

the Holy Spirit.[8] Christ was indignant with their accusation, for every miracle He worked was done firstly in the name of the Father, secondly by the power of His own divinity, and thirdly through the Holy Spirit. He tells them, "If I cast out demons with the finger of God, surely the kingdom of God has come upon you," and the Church Fathers taught that the finger of God was the Spirit Himself.[9] He also told the crowds, "The words that I speak to you are spirit, and they are life;"[10] so even His teaching and theology were imbued with the Holy Spirit.

The Fathers considered a person's obedience to the commands of the Gospel as proof that the person was indwelt by the Spirit. They also said the power contained in an evangelical command could be unleashed by simply saying it. For example, uttering the words, "Lord Jesus Christ, Son of God, have mercy on me, a sinner," gives a person the power and authority to expel the dark shadows that lurk in the mind. This is why the Church still believes till today (and I firmly believe it) that the tenacious adherence to the commands of the Bible brings victory in life.

✛ ✛ ✛

Now, let us go deeper. Pay close attention. On the Day of Pentecost, we were granted the Spirit of Christ and the Spirit of the Father; and there, then, is the Holy Trinity. The Resurrection of our Lord from the dead had, firstly, a physical dimension—the body that died and atoned for humanity's sins was returned to life by the Holy Spirit.[11] (So the Resurrection too was accomplished with the Holy Spirit.

8   Mark 3:29
9   See Matt. 12:28.
10 John 6:63
11 Rom. 8:11

And that physical body was in fact our own physical nature.) And that self-same Holy Spirit He has given to us. He rose from the dead by the Spirit, ascended to heaven, sat at the right hand of the Father, then sent us the Spirit.

What a gloriously new and joyful understanding of the Spirit this is! "It is to your advantage that I go away; for if I do not go away, the Helper will not come to you; but if I depart, I will send Him to you."[12] In other words, "If I do not send you the Spirit, then everything I have done would be of benefit only to Me, but not to you all." The point I want to make is this: The Spirit sent by Christ from the Father, the Spirit of the Resurrection, was sent into the world and came and dwelt in the Church that she might lead a life of resurrection. Do you see now the significant link between Resurrection and Pentecost? Do you understand the length and depth and width and height of that sacred relationship?

So since the Day of Pentecost until now, the Spirit immerses us in resurrection life; or, to put it another way, the Spirit makes us live in the presence of the risen Christ. "Where two or three are gathered together in My name, I am there in the midst of them";[13] and His personal presence is effected, of course, by the presence of the Holy Spirit. The Church lives by the power of the Risen Lord; and she did not begin to utter the cry, "Christ is Risen!" until after she had received the Holy Spirit. So while the philosophers and scholars we alluded to earlier are darkening the life of mankind, the Spirit is delivering it from death to life. As Revelation says, "Blessed and holy *is* he who has part in the first resurrection. Over such the second death has no power."[14] The first resurrection is our present life in Christ Jesus and our participation in the Church. Any believer who dies

---

12 John 16:7
13 Matt. 18:20
14 Rev. 20:6

gets immediately transported into the resurrection glory. The second death can never swallow him who lives in Christ.

All these reflections generate in us a strong thirst for the Holy Spirit. As this evening's Gospel says so beautifully, "If anyone thirsts, let him come to Me and drink. Whoever believes in Me, as the Scripture has said, 'Out of his heart will flow rivers of living water.' Now this He said about the Spirit, whom those who believed in Him were to receive."[15] This is actual *thirst*, and it is quenched by *drinking*. But what if a person does not thirst? He will not drink. And if he does not drink? Living water will not flow out of him. Beloved, I must tell you something that grieves me deeply: We are not drinking. But this drinking is absolutely essential! And so, thirst for Christ and for the Holy Spirit is the very essence of life. It is the essence of Christianity. I see this thirst so scarcely in us, and yet it ought to be our whole aim in life!

"If anyone thirsts, let him come to Me and drink." Drink *freely*! It does not require gold or silver or anything else. The apostles were praying together with one mind when the Holy Spirit descended upon them; the vital criterion for the Spirit's presence is *fellowship*. The saints of old used to say there is no salvation outside the Church. Salvation is not gained in isolation. This is contrary to the thinking of the charismatics, who say the Spirit is given to a person for his personal advantage. No, the Spirit is given to a person for the good of the whole Church. Anyone who receives a gift of the Spirit, but does not unite it with the Church, dies. Spiritual gifts do not guarantee a person's salvation. This idea doesn't come from me, but from the Bible: "'Lord, Lord, have we not prophesied in Your name, cast out demons in Your name, and done many wonders in Your name?'" And the shocking response: "'I never knew you; depart from Me, you who practice lawlessness!'"[16] *Lawlessness!* So, the receiving of gifts requires

15 John 7:37, 38
16 Matt. 7:21–23

a person to live and unite with others. An isolated and a segregated lifestyle is a sign of disease, not of health.

I want to comment on the principle that the Bible does not allow any redemptive event to occur without a prior prophecy. Our Lord's sufferings were pre-announced;[17] His death with its various details was pre-announced;[18] the burial in the tomb and its duration was pre-announced;[19] the Resurrection, the Ascension, and Pentecost were all likewise pre-announced.[20] The time fails me to prove these points separately, but it is your personal duty to read the Bible and find out these things on your own.

Each of the Gospels speaks about the Holy Spirit, but the Gospel of John most of all. He devotes three entire chapters to the Spirit, describing His work, His methods, and His blessings.[21] Per the teachings of Christ, therefore, the Holy Spirit constitutes a vitally foundational part of the Gospel message. In speaking about the full range of God's redemptive work in the Bible, we today place the seal on our discussion with Pentecost—thus revealing the great majesty of the Holy Spirit's work.

Behold the majesty of the Gospel: for by prophecy, the Gospel was written in life before it was written by pen; or, more pointedly, the Gospel was *lived* before it was *written down*. By prophecy, the Gospel was announced and expounded before it ever came to be. Not a single other book in this world can make such a boast. Our amazement in the Bible is not just in the words it speaks, but in the action it achieves. It promises and forecasts future events long before they ever begin to occur. See the power of the Bible! The last step in this dramatic chain of events is the work of the Holy Spirit, which was

---

17 E.g., Is. 53
18 E.g., Ps. 22
19 E.g., Matt. 12:40
20 Ps. 16:10; Dan. 7; Joel 2
21 Chs. 14—16

foretold in detail centuries before it came to pass. "You shall receive power when the Holy Spirit has come upon you; and you shall be witnesses to Me in Jerusalem, and in all Judea and Samaria, and to the end of the earth."[22] It all came to pass.

This Bible we read really defies description. And it defies history too. I get very agitated with the number of books coming out of the press these days talking about "the historical Jesus." The idea makes me utter an incredulous laugh. Christ has changed all of history! He came at the end of days, and who can endure the day of the Lord?[23] In God's prophecies, the Bible transcends this world and joins time to eternity. This is not mere history that we read; it is not the words of mere men. It is God Himself speaking directly to us: "God, who at various times and in various ways spoke in time past to the fathers by the prophets, has in these last days *spoken to us by His Son*."[24] Man's word is just history in time. God's Word blends time with eternity itself. If God speaks, close your eyes, ignore the clock, and listen to the Word that shakes heaven and earth, but which itself can never be shaken.

✛ ✛ ✛

Let us take things a little more slowly now in our discussion. I have spoken before about the Spirit's role in our talents and gifts and service in this world, that is, the practical side of His work. But now I will speak specifically about His role in our salvation. This is a *mystical* truth that tends to escape our notice most of the time; but on this evening, let us delve fully into it.

When Christ became incarnate, the divine and human natures

---

22 Acts 1:8
23 Mal. 3:2
24 Heb. 1:1

joined to form a complete union. His divinity united with the flesh He took from the Virgin, and the result was a single *hypostasis* or *prosopon*. On the outside, Christ did not *appear* to the disciples to be a combination of divine and human natures. He was just a human being. This is what caused their shock at His words about eating His flesh and drinking His blood. His union with humanity was personal and individual, not collective. I mean that He became a single human with a single body; He didn't seize all humans and squeeze them into a single human "mass" (like a great ball of dough) and unite with that. (Sometimes we wish He had done so in order to make man's salvation a finished matter. But rather, He remains patient and desires to save us one-by-one, by our faith.)

Now at Christ's death, that body taken from the Virgin, as a human body, bore the sins of all humanity, which made it susceptible to death. So far, so good. But what now? How do I benefit from that transaction? I don't even understand very well the concept of His taking my sin upon Himself. He then rose from the dead, and many saw Him—very well, but what is that to me? All this is happening to *Him*, as an individual hypostasis, or as an isolated being.

But here we come to the point: Once Christ ascended to heaven and sent down the Holy Spirit to Earth, that Spirit of the Resurrection came to dwell in each one of us. He lives now inside Abba Luke, Abba Cornelius, Abba Peshoy, and everyone else sitting around me. We have all received the Spirit of Christ—we have not the Spirit of Jesus who died, but of Jesus who rose. And since we are given the gift of the Resurrection, we may die to the world. It is not the other way around. Christ died in the world, then rose again; but we first receive the Spirit of resurrection and then die to the world. I hope you all understand now the grandeur of the Spirit's work. By receiving the Spirit into your life, you become participants in Christ's suffering, death, Resurrection, Ascension, and enthronement at the Father's right hand.

Christ's Resurrection is activated in the world, or is made capable of regenerating the world, solely by the mediation of the Holy Spirit. This is why Christ breathed on the disciples: in order to grant the Spirit to the Church; that is, to bequeath *Himself* to the Church. Peter and the apostles immediately began baptizing people, according to their role as the new representatives of Christ, because they now had Christ's own Spirit. He told them, "All authority has been given to Me in heaven and on earth. Go therefore and make disciples of all the nations, baptizing them in the name of the Father and of the Son and of the Holy Spirit."[25] They began to baptize because they were the physical delegates of the Christ, who alone baptizes.

I have repeatedly insisted on the point that the priest does not baptize except by *delegation*. The priest immerses the candidate with his own hands, but it is in reality Christ who is baptizing. I did not invent this doctrine; the church fathers speak about it profusely, and St. Basil most among them. "I did not know Him, but He who sent me to baptize with water said to me, 'Upon whom you see the Spirit descending, and remaining on Him, this is He who baptizes with the Holy Spirit.'"[26] Christ is the sole figure who can baptize by the Holy Spirit. Neither bishop, nor priest, nor angel, nor any other person can do it—these all receive only a delegated efficacy from Christ. The *officiating* minister dunks the person, saying, "I baptize you in the name of the Father, the Son, and the Holy Spirit," but the *real* minister is Christ.

It's obvious, then, what a gigantic leap the disciples took at Pentecost—how new a nature and immense a power they received. They began to resemble Christ in their words, their conduct, and their miracles. "Most assuredly, I say to you, he who believes in Me, the works

---

25 Luke 28:18
26 John 1:33

that I do he will do also; and greater works than these he will do."[27] In other words, beginning on the Day of Pentecost, the Church began to do the work of Christ Himself; and the Holy Spirit is finishing His work of salvation.

I want to mention a verse that will tie these ideas together and make them powerful realities: God has "begotten us again to a living hope."[28] Do you possess a *living* hope? A living hope is one that never dies, is never moved, is never quenched, and never slackens. *You* might weaken, and age, and crawl about on your belly, and need to be carried about as an invalid—but your hope all the while remains firm within. The body may perish, but hope never perishes! He has "begotten us again to a living hope *through the resurrection of Jesus Christ from the dead*."[29] When Christ rose from the dead, human nature also rose to a new way of life, utterly different from the old. This second birth is a gift of Christ's Resurrection.

Now someone might say, "I want all this. I want this hope and that blessing and the Christ you keep talking about!" But none of these things can be received without the Holy Spirit's entrance into your life. Every baptism that happens to every individual is a real, actual, living repetition of Pentecost. And each baptized individual is no longer the child of the Adam made of dust, but of the Christ risen on the third day. The very presence of the Holy Spirit at baptism is exactly equal to His presence at Pentecost, and there is not an atom of inequality in power or gifts bestowed by the Spirit between the two events.

You may then say to me, "In that case, Abba—hallelujah! I'm baptized and I've received the new nature." I respond that it is all good

---

27   John 14:12
28   1 Pet. 1:3
29   1 Pet. 1:3

and well, but another verse must be borne in mind in order to avoid distorting the whole truth. The verse is this: "If the Spirit of Him who raised Jesus from the dead dwells in you, He who raised Christ from the dead will also give life to your mortal bodies through His Spirit who dwells in you."[30] In other words, if the Spirit resides within you, you will feel His strength surging through your members. How so, you ask? Hear the following verse: "If by the Spirit you put to death the deeds of the body, you will live."[31]

This is the assurance, the guarantee, the "keystone" of the Spirit's presence within you. (When workers are constructing a brick arch, the keystone is the critical supporter of the entire structure; and when the arch is complete, the scaffolding is removed, and the entire structure stands erect by the support of the keystone.) This does not mean that if you possess the Holy Spirit you are invincible to sin. Rather, it means that the indwelling of the Holy Spirit gives us new spiritual powers—greater than our domineering wills, greater than our unbending intellects, and stronger than the apathy of this weak body.

Again, the Holy Spirit does not render us invincible to sin. The gifts of the Spirit—apostolicity, prophecy, teaching, authority, interpretation, tongues, healings, and whatever else—are *not* safeguards against sin. In fact, the opposite is true. We learn from church history that every individual who was granted a large portion of these gifts was put in danger of a sudden fall. It is hazardous to receive spiritual abilities beyond the normal abilities of one's natural self. When a person can raise the dead, the temptation to self-conceit and self-reliance is serious.

They once asked a saint who had just raised a dead man, "What were your feelings during the miracle?" He replied, "I felt as though

---

30   Rom. 8:11
31   Rom. 8:13

the edge of a sword were placed at my throat, and if I moved an inch to the left or right, my neck would be instantly severed." He wasn't joyful and elated at the miracle, because he knew the devil was at his side threatening him. The Holy Spirit thus does not shield a person from sin, but He grants him the power to make war against it, and ultimately guarantees *victory*. He is the pledge of your victory. Depend on Him, and you cannot fail. But neglect Him, forget about Him, fail to petition His aid and to surrender your whole mind to His leading, and sin will crouch at your door.[32]

It is not a small thing to be given the weapons of victory and to receive the capacity to overcome the obstacles of life. See how great it is when the Spirit dwells in a person! He gives him the life of the Resurrection and makes him a member of Christ's own Body. But let us not forget the unfortunate example of Peter. He was a representative of the Circumcision[33] and was one day sitting at a meal with a group of Gentile Christians, until he was told that a group of believers were coming down from Jerusalem.[34] He immediately hurried the Gentiles into a room by themselves, while he sat alone with his plate before him as if he had been eating in solitude all along.

Paul, however, was present at the scene, and he called Peter's action

---

32 Gen. 4:7

33 "The Circumcision" is a technical term used in the New Testament to indicate Jewish Christians. Even after coming to faith in Christ, they continued to adhere to the requirements and duties of Moses' Law. An example of this is Peter and John's trip to the temple to pray (Acts 3:1), whereas a Gentile Christian would have never considered approaching the temple for religious worship. Some of the Circumcision thus erroneously considered Gentile Christians to be unclean or somehow inferior to Jewish believers; hence, Peter's embarrassment at being seen eating with them upon the arrival of the Jewish believers from Jerusalem.

34 Gal. 2:11–14

into question. At the time Paul was lesser than Peter; for Peter was in fact the eldest of the apostles, both in age and experience, in addition to possessing the toughest personality. "What is this you're doing, Peter? Are you acting the hypocrite?" But now where is the Holy Spirit, you may ask? This Peter raised the dead; wasn't it he who said, "Tabitha, rise"?[35] Can someone who raises the dead act like a hypocrite? Yes, because he lost his focus, and *he feared*.

Oh, woe to man when he *fears!* O my beloved, my son, my friend in life, I say to you: *Do not fear*. Do *not* fear! Have fear neither of today, nor of tomorrow, nor of disease, nor of death; fear neither hunger, nor thirst, nor Satan, nor war. Because once fear enters you, the devil will exploit it that very instant and drag you about wherever he wants. In Revelation, in the list of those who are cast out,[36] the first mentioned are "the cowardly." And why should we fear anything? We are given victory over death. We are given the Holy Spirit, by whom we may defeat everything in this world.

Please remember that I am not just speaking to you empty words. This is not a mere religious sermon. I have said before and say again now that I am neither preacher, nor hierarch, nor abbot, nor any other person of consequence in the Church. I am not a father to wield paternal authority over you; I trust in God as the Father of us all. I am simply a monk, and I will die simply a monk. What gives me the boldness to sit and speak before you today is the fact that I have lived and tasted the things that I describe. To neglect the transfer of such things to you would become a judgment upon me. Since I have personally felt the Holy Spirit's power in these things, I need not preach to you; my duty is just to bequeath a feeling, an experience, a way of living to you. "God has not given us a spirit of fear, but of power and of

---

35　Acts 9:40
36　Rev. 21:8

love and of a sound mind."[37] This is the spirit of the Resurrection, not the spirit of weariness and regret and slumber. Can we all *wake up*, Abbas? "Awake, you who sleep; arise from the dead, and Christ will give you light."[38] You have been given the Spirit of victory and glory!

37   2 Tim. 1:7
38   Eph. 5:14

Ancient Faith Publishing hopes you have enjoyed and benefited from this book. The proceeds from the sales of our books only partially cover the costs of operating our nonprofit ministry—which includes both the work of **Ancient Faith Publishing** and the work of **Ancient Faith Radio.** Your financial support makes it possible to continue this ministry both in print and online. Donations are tax-deductible and can be made at www.ancientfaith.com.

To request a catalog of other publications,
please call us at (800) 967-7377 or (219) 728-2216
or log onto our website: **store.ancientfaith.com**

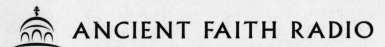

ANCIENT FAITH RADIO

Bringing you Orthodox Christian music, readings,
prayers, teaching, and podcasts 24 hours a day since 2004 at
www.ancientfaith.com